BEING LOGICAL

Being Logical

A
GUIDE
to
GOOD
THINKING

D. Q. McInerny

RANDOM HOUSE TRADE PAPERBACKS ⬟ NEW YORK

2005 Random House Trade Paperback Edition

Copyright © 2004 by D. Q. McInerny

Published in the United States by Random House Trade Paperbacks,
an imprint of The Random House Publishing Group,
a division of Random House, Inc., New York.

RANDOM HOUSE TRADE PAPERBACKS and colophon are
trademarks of Random House, Inc.

Originally published in hardcover in the United States by
Random House, an imprint of The Random House
Publishing Group, a division of Random House, Inc., in 2004.

LIBRARY OF CONGRESS CATALOGING-IN-PUBLICATION DATA
McInerny, D. Q.
Being logical : a guide to good thinking / D. Q. McInerny.
p.   cm.
Includes bibliographical references.
ISBN 0-8129-7115-9
1. Logic.   2. Reasoning.   3. Thought and thinking.   I. Title.

BC71.M37 2004
160—dc22   2003058779

Printed in the United States of America

www.atrandom.com

22 24 26 28 29 27 25 23 21

Text design by Mary A. Wirth

IN MEMORIAM

AUSTIN CLIFFORD MCINERNY
and
VIVIAN GERTRUDE RUSH MCINERNY

We may take Fancy for a companion,
but must follow Reason as our guide.

—DR. SAMUEL JOHNSON

Preface

LOGIC IS ABOUT clear and effective thinking. It is a science and an art. This book is intended to introduce readers to the rudiments of the science as well as to the basic skills associated with the art.

We all know people who are very bright but who do not always shine when it comes to being logical. They have the ability to think logically—that is, clearly and effectively—but that ability does not habitually manifest itself. The likelihood is that it has never been properly developed, pointing to a deficiency in their education. Indeed, logic is the very backbone of a true education, and yet it is seldom taught as such in American schools. To my mind, logic is the missing piece of the American educational system, the subject that informs every other subject from English to history to science and math.

Some readers, especially if this book represents their first serious encounter with logic, might react skittishly to what appears to be an overly technical vocabulary, or to the symbolic notation that logic makes frequent use of. Don't be scared off by initial impressions. I have made a concerted effort to present whatever technical matters I deal with here (which in any event are not all that trying) in as simple and uncomplicated a way as possible. At the same time, however, I have tried to avoid lapsing into the simplistic. A dumbed-down logic is not logic at all. Other readers might be put off by what they perceive to be an emphasis upon the obvious. I do, in fact, place a good deal of stress on the obvious in this book, and that is quite deliberate. In logic, as in life, it is the obvious that most often bears emphasizing, because it so easily escapes our notice. If I have belabored certain points, and regularly opted for the explicit over the implicit, it is because I adhere to the time-honored pedagogic principle that it is always safest to assume as little as possible.

Logic, taken as a whole, is a wide, deep, and wonderfully varied field, and I would be pleased if my readers, as a result of their encounter with this little book, were moved to become more familiar with it. However, my aim here is very modest. This is neither a treatise in logical theory nor a textbook in logic—though I would not be disappointed to learn that it proves useful in the classroom. My governing purpose was to write a practical guidebook, presenting the basic principles of logic in a way that is accessible to those who are encountering the subject for the first time. *Being Logical* seeks to produce practitioners, not theoreticians—people for whom knowing the principles of logic is in the service of being logical.

In the hope of better serving the practical ends of the book, I have adopted a somewhat informal style, often addressing the reader directly, and, in the manner of a tutor or coach, sometimes assuming a distinctively directive tone. I treat logic in five stages, represented by the five parts of the book, each successive stage building upon the one that preceded it. Part One is preparatory, and deals with the proper frame of mind that must be established if logical thinking is to take place at all. In Parts Two and Three, the heart of the book, we pass into the realm of logic proper. Part Two explains the foundational truths that govern logical thinking, while Part Three focuses on argument—the public expression of logical thinking. In Part Four, I discuss attitudes and frames of mind that promote illogical thinking. Finally, Part Five concentrates on the particulars of illogical thinking—the fallacies.

A final word, of admiration and appreciation, for a sparkling little book called *The Elements of Style*, by William Strunk, Jr., and E. B. White, which was the inspiration for *Being Logical*. What I have managed to accomplish here is no match for the unique achievement of Strunk and White, but I hope that *Being Logical* might to some degree succeed in doing for the cause of good thinking what *The Elements of Style* has done for that of good writing. My earnest wish is that this book may succeed in convincing its readers of the intrinsic importance of logic—and that it engender in them an appreciation for the priceless satisfaction which inevitably accompanies the happy state of being logical.

Contents

PART ONE

Preparing the Mind for Logic

Being logical presupposes our having a sensitivity to language and a knack for its effective use, for logic and language are inseparable. It also presupposes our having a healthy respect for the firm factualness of the world in which we live, for logic is about reality. Finally, being logical presupposes a lively awareness of how the facts that are our ideas relate to the facts that are the objects in the world, for logic is about truth. In this first part of the book I will discuss those attitudes, points of view, and practical procedures whose adoption prepares the mind for a successful engagement with logic.

1. Be Attentive

Many mistakes in reasoning are explained by the fact that we are not paying sufficient attention to the situation in which we find ourselves. This is especially true in familiar situations. That very familiarity causes us to make careless judgments about facts right before our eyes. We misread a situation because we are skimming it, when what we should be doing is perusing it. Often, we assume that a familiar situation will be but a repeat performance of a similar situation we've experienced before. But, in the strictest sense, there are no repeat performances. Every situation is unique, and we must be alert to its uniqueness.

The phrase "to pay attention" is telling. It reminds us

that attention costs something. Attention demands an active, energetic response to every situation, to the persons, places, and things that make up the situation. It is impossible to be truly attentive and passive at the same time. Don't just look, see. Don't just hear, listen. Train yourself to focus on details. The little things are not to be ignored, for it is just the little things that lead us to the big things.

2. Get the Facts Straight

A fact is something made or done. It has clear objective status. It is something we respond to as having an independent status all its own. It is naggingly persistent, demands recognition, and can be nasty if ignored.

There are two basic types of objective facts, things and events. A "thing" is an actually existing entity, animal, vegetable, or mineral. The White House is an example of the first type of fact, and the assassination of Abraham Lincoln of the second. The first type is more basic than the second because events are made up of things or of the actions of things. A state dinner is to be held at the White House. Such an event could not take place were it not for the existence, first and foremost, of the fact that is the White House, and countless other facts as well. In order to establish the factualness of an event, any number of concrete things need to be appealed to.

To determine the reality of a fact that is a thing, all you need do is pay it a visit. If it actually exists it must be somewhere, and, assuming its place to be accessible to you, you can verify its factualness by direct observation. Take the case of the White House. To ascertain its being a fact, rather than purely imaginary, you can travel to Washington, D.C., and there see the White House with your own eyes. That is the most direct and reliable way to establish its factualness. But you could also rely on indirect evidence: For example, by taking the word of a trustworthy eyewitness that the White House is indeed in Washington, D.C. Or you could decide that photographic evidence is sufficient to establish factualness.

But what about an event like Lincoln's assassination? We say that is a fact. What is the justification for that claim? It is an event that is over and done with, and there are no living witnesses to the event whom we might consult. Obviously, we did not ourselves witness the event, so direct evidence is out of the question. In this case our approach will be to acquaint ourselves with a variety of things that serve as indirect evidence of the event. For example, we would consult official documents (police reports, the death certificate, etc.), newspaper accounts, photographs, memoirs, diaries, and items in the *Congressional Record*, all of which are facts in their own right and whose only reasonable explanation is the factualness of Lincoln's assassination. On the basis of the factualness of these things, we establish the factualness of the event. And we thus establish a historical fact.

Facts can also be thought of as objective or subjective. Both things and events are objective facts. They exist in the public domain and are in principle accessible to all. A subjective fact is one that is limited to the subject experiencing it. A headache would be an example of a subjective fact. If I am the one experiencing the headache, then I have direct evidence of its factualness. But if it is you experiencing the headache, I can establish its factualness only indirectly. I must take your word that you have a headache. Establishing the reality of subjective facts depends entirely on the trustworthiness of those who claim to be experiencing them.

To sum up how we get the facts straight: If a given fact is an actually existing thing to which we have access, then the surest way to establish its factualness is to put ourselves in its presence. We then have direct evidence of it. If we cannot establish factualness by direct evidence, we must rigorously test the authenticity and reliability of whatever indirect evidence we appeal to so that, on the basis of that evidence, we can confidently establish the factualness of the thing.

There are only a very limited number of significant public events which we can experience directly. This means that, in almost every case, we must rely on indirect evidence. In establishing the factualness of events by indirect evidence, we must exercise the same kind of care we do in establishing the factualness of "things" by indirect evidence. It all comes down to the authenticity and reliability of our sources.

A subjective fact, to the subject experiencing it, is self-evident under normal circumstance. However, through such mechanisms as self-delusion or rationalization, a person could fail to get straight a fact even about himself.

Because the establishment of the factualness of a subjective fact pertaining to another person depends entirely on the trustworthiness of that person, you must first, insofar as it is possible, establish the trustworthiness of the person in question.

3. Ideas and the Objects of Ideas

Every idea in the mind is ultimately traceable to a thing, or things, actually existing in a world that is independent of and apart from the mind. An idea is the subjective evocation of an objective fact. Clear ideas, then, are ideas that faithfully reflect the objective order from which they derive. Unclear ideas, conversely, are those that give us a distorted representation of the objective world.

Though the control we have over our ideas is not absolute, it is real. This means that we are not helpless in the face of unclear ideas. To ensure that our ideas are clear, we must vigilantly attend to the relationship between any given idea and its object. If it is a strained relationship, if the connection between the idea and its object is tenuous, then we are dealing with an unclear idea.

It is wrong to suppose that because we know things in the world only through our ideas, it is only our ideas which we really know. Our ideas are the means, not the ends, of our knowledge. They link us to the world. If they are clear ideas, the links are strong. The most efficient way to clarify our ideas is to look *through* them to the objects they represent.

4. Be Mindful of the Origins of Ideas

We all tend to favor our own ideas, which is natural enough. They are, after all, in a sense our very own babies, the conceptions of our minds. But conception is possible in the thinking subject only because of the subject's encounter with the world. Our ideas owe their existence, ultimately, to things outside and independent of the mind, to which they refer: objective facts.

Our ideas are clear, and our understanding of them is clear, only to the extent that we keep constant tabs on the things to which they refer. The focus must always be on the originating sources of our ideas in the objective world. We do not really understand our own ideas if we suppose them to be self-generating, that is, not owing their existence to extramental realities.

The more we focus on our ideas in a way that systematically ignores their objective origins, the more unreliable those ideas become. The healthy bonds that bind together the subjective and objective orders are put under great strain, and if we push the process too far, the bonds may break. Then we have effectively divorced ourselves from the objective world. Instead of seeing the world as it is, we see a projected world, one that is not presented *to* our minds but which is the product *of* our minds.

When we speak of "establishing a fact," we do not refer to establishing the existence of an idea in the mind. The idea in the mind, as we have seen, is a subjective fact, but the kind of fact we are concerned with establishing is an objective fact. To do so, we must look beyond our ideas to their sources in the objective world. I establish a fact if I successfully ascertain that there is, for a particular idea I have in mind, a corresponding reality external to my mind. For instance, I have a particular idea in my mind, which I label "cat." Corresponding to that idea are actually existing things in the extramental world called "cats." But I could have another idea in my mind, which I label "centaur" but for which no corresponding fact can be found in the extramental world. For all that, the idea of "centaur" is a subjective fact, since it really exists as an idea in my mind.

5. Match Ideas to Facts

There are three basic components to human knowledge: first, an objective fact (e.g., a cat); second, the idea of a cat; third, the word we apply to the idea, allowing us to communicate it to others (e.g., in English, "cat"). It all starts with the cat. If there were no real cats, there would be no idea about them, and there would be no word for the idea. I have been stressing the general point that ideas (subjective realities) are clear or sound to the extent that they reflect objective realities. And we have said that all ideas have their ultimate source in the objective world. Now we must look more closely at how ideas relate to the objective world, for the relation is not always simple. Next, we must address the question: How are bad ideas possible?

Sometimes there is a direct correlation between an idea and an objective fact. Example: the idea of cat. We will call this a "simple" idea. Corresponding to my idea of cat is a single, particular sort of entity in the extramental world— that furry, purring creature which in English we name a cat. In dealing with simple ideas it is relatively easy to test their reliability, because we need only refer to one thing. My idea of cat is clear and sound if it refers to an actual cat.

We will call "complex" ideas those for which there is no simple one-to-one correspondence between idea and thing. Here the correspondence is one to many. There is more than a single originating source for this kind of idea in the objective world. Let's take the idea of democracy. Is it a clear or a sound one? It is, at least potentially. It is a clear or sound idea to the extent that we are able to relate it to the objective world. But there are many things in the objective world that go together to compose the rich meaning of the idea of democracy: persons, events, constitutions, legislative acts, past institutions, present institutions. If my idea of democracy is going to be communicable to others, it must refer to what is common to me and to others, those many things in the objective world that are its originating source. To prevent my idea from being a product of pure subjectivism, in which case it could not be communicated to others, I must continuously touch base with those many facts in the objective world from which the idea was born.

How are we to explain bad (that is, unclear or unsound) ideas? An idea is unclear or unsound to the degree that it is distanced from and unmindful of its originating source in the objective world. No idea, even the most bizarre, can completely sever its ties with the objective world, but ideas can become so remote from that world that their relation to it is difficult, if not impossible, to see. Bad ideas can be informative, not about the objective world—for they have ceased faithfully to reflect that world—but about the subjective state of the persons who nourish those ideas. Bad ideas do not just happen. We are responsible for them. They result from carelessness on our part, when we cease to pay sufficient attention to the relational quality of ideas, or, worse, are a product of the willful rejection of objective facts.

6. Match Words to Ideas

As we have seen, first comes the thing, then the idea, then the word. If our ideas are sound to the extent that they faithfully represent the thing, they will be clearly communicable only if we clothe them in words that accurately signify them. Ideas as such are not communicable from one mind to another. They have to be carefully fitted to words, so that the words might communicate them faithfully. Putting the right word to an idea is not an automatic process, and sometimes it can be quite challenging. We have all had the experience of knowing what we want to say but not being able to come up with the words for it.

How do we ensure that our words are adequate to the ideas they seek to convey? The process is essentially the same as the one we follow when confirming the clarity and soundness of our ideas: We must go back to the sources of the ideas. Often we cannot come up with the right word for an idea because we don't have a firm grasp on the idea itself. Usually, when we clarify the idea by checking it against its source in the objective world, the right word will come to us.

Sometimes there is a perfect match between word and idea, which would mean a perfect match between word and thing, for if the idea is clear it faithfully represents the thing, and if the word accurately expresses the idea, it would at the same time faithfully identify the thing. This commonly happens with simple ideas. If I say, "The monument is granite," and the monument to which I refer is in fact granite, then in "granite" I have the perfect match for the idea and the thing it represents. It gets more complicated when we are dealing with complex ideas, but the general principle remains the same: In order to guarantee accuracy in your use of words, go back to the objective facts that are the foundational explanations for words.

In the effort to come up with words that accurately convey ideas, our ultimate purpose should always be this: to so shape our language that it communicates to others the way things actually are—objective reality. It is not enough that language be satisfied with ideas as such, but with clear and sound ideas. Let us say I fervently hold to the real existence of Lilliput, and have all sorts of ideas about it. I may be able to come up with scads of words that accurately convey those ideas to you, but all those words do is reveal the state of my mind. They do not reveal the state of the world. They deal with subjective reality, not objective reality.

7. *Effective Communication*

Language and logic are inextricably bound up with each other. How that is so becomes clear when we recall the relationship between the idea and the word. Although it is a disputed point among the experts, it seems possible that we can hold an idea in our mind without having a precise word for it. In any event, if we are going to attempt to communicate an idea to others, it is imperative that we express it by a word. And, as we have seen, the better the fit between word and idea, the clearer and more effective the communication of the idea.

Matching words to ideas is the first and most basic step in communication. The next step is putting ideas together to form coherent statements. If I said to you "dog" or "cat," your response would be expectant, waiting to hear more. You would wonder, What about dogs or cats? Through the words I'm speaking, you know the ideas I'm dealing with, but you don't know what I intend to do with those ideas. I'm simply "saying" the ideas; I'm not saying anything *about* them. We say something about ideas when we put them together to form statements that can be responded to affirmatively or negatively. Notice that if someone simply says "dog," there would not be much sense in responding with "That's true" or "That's false." But if someone says something about a dog—"The dog is in the garage"—then such a response would be appropriate. "Statement" has a special meaning in logic. It is a linguistic expression to which the response of either "true" or "false" is appropriate.

Words have been called the building blocks of language, but it is the *statement* that logic starts with, for it is only at the level of the statement that the question of truth or falsity is introduced, and logic is all about establishing what is true and distinguishing it from what is false. It can sometimes be tough enough determining whether a statement is true or false when that statement is clearly understood. But if we have difficulty understanding what a statement is attempting to say, then our difficulties are compounded, because we have to figure out the meaning of the statement before we can get on to the main business of determining whether it is true or false. Thus the importance of clear, effective communication.

It is impossible to have clear communication without clear thinking. How can I give you a clear idea of something if it is not first clear in my own mind? However, clear ideas do not guarantee clear communication. I may have a perfectly good idea of what I'm *trying* to say, but can't succeed in getting my ideas across clearly and effectively.

Here are some basic guidelines for effective communication:

Don't assume your audience understands your meaning if you don't make it explicit.

The more complicated the subject matter dealt with, the more important this point is. We sometimes take it for granted that an audience is aware of background information that is necessary for a correct understanding of the subject we're speaking on, but in fact the audience may be quite innocent of this information. When in doubt, spell out the background information. It is always better to err on the side of saying too much than on the side of saying too little.

Speak in complete sentences.

The sentence with which logic is most concerned is the declarative sentence. A declarative sentence is the same thing as a statement (also called a "proposition" in logic). If I say "Dog turtle," "Falling stock prices in July," "The building's Indiana limestone facade," you could presume I am intending in each case to link certain ideas together, but you do not know how. That is because I am not forming genuine statements. I need to speak in complete sentences: "The dog bit the turtle," "Falling stock prices in July depressed Julian," "The building's Indiana limestone facade was severely defaced by the vandals."

Don't treat evaluative statements as if they were statements of objective fact.

"The Pearce Building is on the corner of Main and Adams" is a statement of objective fact, and as such it is either true or false. "The Pearce Building is ugly" is an evaluative statement, and as such it combines both subjective and objective elements. Evaluative statements do not lend themselves to a simple true-or-false response. We must not invite unwarranted responses to statements, which is just what we do when we attempt to pass off an evaluative statement as if it were a statement of objective fact. True statements of objective fact are not open to argument; evaluative statements are. If I want an evaluative statement to be accepted, I must argue for it.

Avoid double negatives.

In Spanish, double negatives have the effect of intensifying the negative import of a sentence. In English, double negatives cancel each other out, making the sentence affirmative. This can sometimes cause confusion, since the sentence sounds negative but is in fact affirmative. To avoid that confusion, and for greater clarity of expression, avoid double negatives. Instead of saying, "It is not unlikely that she would be welcome," say "She would be welcome."

Gear your language to your audience.

If you are a physicist discussing the principle of indeterminacy with other physicists at a professional conference, you can freely use the technical jargon of your profession. But if you are asked to explain that principle to a group of nonphysicists, you should adjust your vocabulary and present your material in ordinary language. Don't use technical or "insider" language merely to impress people. The point is to communicate. The two extremes to be avoided are talking down to people and talking over their heads.

An important point to note here is that we obviously cannot attune our language to our audience if we do not know our audience. The first order of business, then, is to have a reasonably good sense of the composition and background of the group you will be addressing.

8. *Avoid Vague and Ambiguous Language*

Vagueness and ambiguity are specific instances of the kind of language that can inhibit clear and effective communication. The word "vague" comes from the Latin adjective *vagus*, which means "wandering," while the word "ambiguous" traces its origin to the Latin verb *ambigere*, which means "to wander about." Vague and ambiguous words and expressions wander about among various ideas instead of settling definitely upon one or another particular idea. They all share the defect of not having a fixed, unmistakable meaning.

A word is vague if its referent is blurred. We do not know precisely what the word is pointing to. Consider the two statements "People don't like music like that" and "They say he will not run for a second term." A natural response to the first statement would be: "What people, and what kind of music?" A response to the second statement might be: "Who are 'they'?" In both instances we are uncertain of what is being talked about for lack of precise information. For those statements substitute these: "People who have been trained at the San Francisco Conservatory of Music don't like West Cork folk music." "The Candidate Selection Committee for the People's Party says he will not run again." Now we have something more definite to respond to.

As a rule, the more general the word, the vaguer it is. A sure preventative against vagueness, then, is to make your words as precise and sharply focused as possible. Your reader or listener should not be forced to guess at exactly what your words are pointing to. If you mean to communicate information specifically about rocking chairs, or antique chairs, or dentist's chairs, or electric chairs, then use those specific terms rather than the more general "chairs." Usually the context in which a general term appears will allow your audience to figure out its referent, but if you have any doubts about that, use a specific term.

Terms like "love," "democracy," "fairness," "equality," "good," and "evil" can be vague, not because they have no meaning but because they are especially rich in meaning. Thus, two people can use the same term—"love," for example—and understand it in quite different, perhaps even contradictory, ways. That is why it is imperative, in using terms of this sort, that you make explicit your understand-

ing of them. Before you attempt to persuade an audience
that a certain situation is unfair, tell them what you mean by
unfairness.

An ambiguous term ("equivocal," in the language of
logic) is one which has more than a single meaning and
whose context does not clearly indicate which meaning is
intended. A sign posted at a fork in a trail which reads BEAR
TO THE RIGHT can be understood in two ways. The more
probable meaning is that it is instructing hikers to take the
right trail, not the left. But let us say that the ranger who
painted the sign meant to say just the opposite. He was trying to warn hikers against taking the right trail because
there is a grizzly bear in the area through which it passes.
The ranger's language was therefore careless, and open to
misinterpretation that could have serious consequences.
The only way to avoid ambiguity is to spell things out as explicitly as possible: "Keep left. Do not use trail to the right.
Grizzly bears in the area."

9. Avoid Evasive Language

You should always be so straightforward in your language
that it would be impossible for any reasonably attentive audience to miss your meaning. This is not to suggest that you
have to use words like sledgehammers. One can be perfectly clear without being either crude or cruel.

There is a place for euphemism in language. But we
have to be careful that euphemistic usage doesn't become a
way of evading what really is at issue. Consider a term like
"final solution," which was used to disguise a heinous pro-

gram for exterminating an entire people. The problem with evasive language, language that does not state directly what a speaker or writer has in mind, is twofold. First, and obviously, it can deceive an audience. Second, and more subtly, it can have a deleterious effect on the people who use it, distorting their sense of reality. The user shapes language, but language shapes the user as well. If we consistently use language that serves to distort reality, we can eventually come to believe our own twisted rhetoric. Such is the power of language. At first hearing, terms like "cultural revolution" and "reeducation" might sound quite harmless. Then one learns that they masked totalitarian brutality at its worst.

It is juvenile to use language simply to shock. But shocking language is preferable to evasive language, if it can disabuse people of hazy ideas and acquaint them with the truth.

10. Truth

The whole purpose of reasoning, of logic, is to arrive at the truth of things. This is often an arduous task, as truth can sometimes be painfully elusive. But not to pursue truth would be absurd, since it is the only thing that gives meaning to all our endeavors. It would be equally absurd to suppose that truth is something forever to be pursued but never to be attained, for that renders our activity purposeless, which is to say, irrational, and turns truth into a chimera.

Truth has two basic forms. There is "ontological" truth and "logical" truth. Of these two, ontological truth is the more basic. By ontological truth we refer to the truth of being or existence. Something is said to be ontologically true, then, if it actually exists; it has real being. The lamp sitting on my desk is ontologically true because it is really there. It is not an illusion. The opposite of ontological truth is nonexistence.

Logical truth, as you might suspect, is the form of truth we are most directly concerned with as logicians. Logical truth is simply the truth of statements. More broadly, we could say that it is truth as it manifests itself in our thinking and language. Let us examine the notion of logical truth carefully, for it is going to prove very important in all that follows.

Recall the definition of a statement, given earlier: a linguistic expression to which the responses "true" or "false" would be appropriate. To affirm a statement is to declare it to be true; to deny it is to brand it as false.

A statement is true if what it says reflects what is the case. Consider the statement "The boat is tied to the pier." The statement is true if there really is a boat, there really is a pier, and the boat is really tied to the pier. What a true statement does is declare, through the medium of language, a correspondence between ideas in the mind (subjective facts) and real states of affairs in the world (objective facts). "The boat is tied to the pier" would be false if there were a discrepancy between what it says and what actually is the case.

Establishing the truth in any particular situation is a matter of determining whether what one believes to be true, or suspects might be true, has a basis in fact. It is a matter of bringing together into harmonious juxtaposition the subjective and the objective. But the focus of attention here must be on the objective order of things. If I am uncertain about the truth of the statement "The dog is in the garage," it will not help me to resolve the issue if all I do is reflect upon my own ideas on dogs and garages and the various ways they can be related to one another. I have to go out and check the garage. It should be clear now why we said that of the two forms of truth, ontological and logical, the former is more basic. What determines the truth or falsity of a statement is what actually exists in the real world. Logical truth, in other words, is founded upon ontological truth.

A word in passing about lies. Lying is more a psychological problem than a logical one. When I lie, I have no doubts about an actually existing situation in the real world, but in my statement about that situation I consciously and deliberately contradict my own knowledge. I know the situation to be properly expressible in the form "A is B," but my statement says "A is not B."

Logical truth, as we have seen, is a matter of a correspondence between the content of a statement (which reflects the ideas held by the person making the statement) and objective facts. This understanding of the nature of truth, not surprisingly, has been called the "correspondence theory of truth." Another theory, the "coherence theory of truth," is subordinate to the correspondence theory.

The coherence theory of truth maintains that any given statement is true if it harmoniously fits into (is coherent with) an already established theory or system of thought. Take, for example, Einstein's Special Theory of Relativity. It is concluded that a particular statement about the nature

of the physical world is true because what it says is consonant with the Special Theory of Relativity. What would
make such a conclusion a logically responsible one is the
fact that the Special Theory of Relativity itself, as a theory,
reflects the way the physical world actually *is*. There is a
correspondence between the theory and objective reality.
We can see, then, that the coherence theory of truth, if responsibly applied, depends upon the correspondence theory of truth, which remains foundational.

We should be aware, though, that the coherence theory
of truth can be seriously abused, which would be the case if
a statement is judged to be true merely by virtue of the fact
that it fits into an established theory or system of thought
that itself does not correspond with reality, or does so only
questionably. For example, if Marxist economic theory can
be shown to be dubious, then the claim that a certain statement about economic matters is true because it is consonant
with that theory is likewise dubious.

PART TWO

The Basic Principles
of Logic

W hether logic is regarded as a science, an art, or a skill—and it can properly be regarded as all three—there must be principles, seminal regulating ideas, that shape the enterprise and guide its activities. In this part we will treat the most basic of the principles of logic. Our focus will be less on the theoretical backdrop of the principles and more on their practical application. The ideal is to assimilate these principles to the point where they become like second nature to you, smoothly guiding your thought without your having to refer consciously to them.

1. First Principles

A science is any organized body of knowledge that is possessed of first principles. The first principles of any science are those fundamental truths upon which the science is founded and by which all its activities are informed. Logic, as a science, has its first principles, but logic stands in a unique relationship to all other sciences because the first principles of logic apply not just to logic but to all the sciences. Indeed, their coverage is more comprehensive still, because they apply to human reason as such, however it might be exercised. This being so, the terms "the first principles of logic" and "the first principles of human reason" can be said to refer to the same thing.

There are four first principles of logic (or of human reason); the one we are most concerned with here is the principle of contradiction. To put it in its proper context, however, let us first review the three other first principles of logic.

THE PRINCIPLE OF IDENTITY

Stated: A thing is what it is.

Explanation: The whole of existing reality is not a homogenous mass. It is a composition of individuals, and the individuals are distinguishable from one another. If a thing is what it is, obviously it is not something other than what it is. An apple is an apple. It is not an orange, a banana, or a pear.

THE PRINCIPLE OF THE EXCLUDED MIDDLE

Stated: Between being and nonbeing there is no middle state.

Explanation: Something either exists or it does not exist; there is no halfway point between the two. The lamp sitting on my desk is either really there or it is not. There is no other possibility. We might ask: How about becoming? Isn't the state of becoming between those of being and nonbeing? The answer is no. There is no such thing as just becoming; there are only *things that become.* The state of becoming is already within the realm of existence. A lamp in the process of being made is not yet a lamp; however, the parts that will go to compose it actually exist, and the lamp's "becoming" depends entirely on their existence. There is, then, no becoming in the absolute sense, no passage from nonbeing to being. Elaine, who is becoming every day a more accomplished musician because of assiduous practice, could not be becoming a musician if she were not already Elaine. There is no becoming with respect to the very existence of a human person. Elaine is "becoming" relatively, not absolutely: She is not becoming Elaine; she is becoming Elaine the more accomplished musician. Again, the basic idea behind the principle of excluded middle is that there are no gaps in being. What we call "becoming" is not a passage from nonbeing to being, but an alteration in a thing or in things already in existence.

THE PRINCIPLE OF SUFFICIENT REASON

Stated: There is a sufficient reason for everything.

Explanation: The principle could also be called "the principle of causality." It states that everything that actually exists in the physical universe has an explanation for its existence. What is implied in the principle is that nothing in the physical universe is self-explanatory or the cause of itself. (For a thing to be a cause of itself, it would somehow have to precede itself, which is absurd.) One thing is said to be the cause of another thing because (a) it explains the very existence of that thing, or (b) it explains why the thing exists in this or that particular way, the "mode" of its existence. Larry's mother and father are the cause of his very existence; if it were not for them, he would not be. Larry's tennis coach in high school is a cause of his being a good tennis player. The coach is the cause of Larry's being in a particular way—in this case, a good tennis player. The coach did not, as did Larry's parents, bring him into being, but he caused a modification in his being. (Of course, there could have been other causes contributing to Larry's being a good tennis player, so the coach may be only one among several causes.)

THE PRINCIPLE OF CONTRADICTION

Stated: It is impossible for something both to be and not be at the same time and in the same respect.

Explanation: This principle could be regarded as a fuller expression of the principle of identity, for if X is X (principle of identity) it cannot at one and the same time be non-X (principle of contradiction). The phrase "in the same respect" in the statement refers to the mode of existence in question. There would be no contradiction if something both was and was not at the same time but in different respects. For example, you can be physically in New York right now and mentally three thousand miles away in San Francisco. But you cannot right now be physically (i.e., in the same respect) both in New York and in San Francisco. Two statements are in contradiction if what one says completely negates what the other says. For example:

a) Alexander Hamilton was a member of George Washington's cabinet.

b) Alexander Hamilton was not a member of George Washington's cabinet.

Both of these statements cannot be true. If one is true, the other must be false, and vice versa. As it happens, (a) is true; (b), therefore, is false.

The word "contradiction" comes from two Latin roots, *contra* ("against") and *dicere* ("to speak"). A contradictory statement in effect speaks against itself, for it is saying something that does not correspond to the objective facts.

The avoidance of contradiction, therefore, is simply the avoidance of falsehood. If the primary purpose of logic is to attain the truth, then it is evident that nothing could be more important than avoiding the opposite of truth.

Sometimes we entertain contradictions without realizing that they are such, because we are ignorant of the relevant objective facts. This is excusable so long as we are not responsible for our ignorance. If we are going to make deliberate statements about important matters in a serious context, we are under obligation to make sure our statements square with what is actually the case. This goes back to the importance of paying attention.

There are times when we hold contradictory views and we know it, at least at one of the deeper levels of consciousness. Most of us could not comfortably live with ourselves if we made a habit of holding flatly contradictory statements at the forefront of our consciousness. For example, I could not explicitly say to myself "I tell many deliberate lies to Stephanie" *and* "I never lie to Stephanie." What I do, assuming the first statement reflects objective facts, is suppress the second statement. Another way I can allow myself to hold on to statements that contradict the facts is deliberately to refrain from examining the facts to which the statements refer. This attitude is expressed by the quip "Don't bother me with the facts; I've already made up my mind." Mental operations of these kinds are not so much instances of reasoning as evasions of reasoning. Obviously, this can have nothing to do with logic. Those forms of unhealthy reasoning can be known as "rationalization." Rationalization is reasoning in the service of falsehood.

Having now reviewed the first principles of reasoning, I am assuming that nothing you just read struck you as radically new. That is because these principles express truths we all become aware of very early in our careers as conscious, rational agents. There are a couple of other things about first principles—all first principles—that need to be noted. They are self-evident. For instance, the first time you read the principle of contradiction, you may have to puzzle over it a moment. But as soon as you see what it is saying, your natural response is, "Of course!"

Another trait of first principles—it follows from their being self-evident—is that they cannot be proven. This means that they are not conclusions that follow from premises; they are not truths dependent upon antecedent truths. This is because first principles represent truths that are absolutely fundamental. They are "first" in the strongest sense of the word.

Consider the principle of sufficient reason. I cannot prove that everything that exists must have a cause, nor do I need to, since it is a truth self-evident to me simply by my observing the way the world works. I either see it or I don't. If the first principles of a science are not seen as self-evident and accepted at face value, the science could not proceed. It would stall right there.

2. Real Gray Areas, Manufactured Gray Areas

A gray area is a situation in which the truth cannot be clearly established. Life is full of them, and they have to be cheer-

fully contended with. But don't make too much of them. Some people become so fixated upon life's gray areas that they eventually succeed in convincing themselves that there is nothing *but* gray areas. A little realism is in order here. We must recognize that many things are, in fact, clearly and sharply defined, and not to see that is simply not to see clearly.

Gray can exist as gray only because there are the distinct alternatives of black and white. That you might find yourself at times in a situation in which you see no clear alternatives does not mean, objectively considered, that there *are* no clear alternatives. It simply means that you do not see them. Don't project your subjective state of uncertainty upon the world at large and claim objective status for it.

To be in a state of uncertainty concerning the truth is neither a pleasant nor a desirable state to be in, and we should always be striving to get out of such states as soon as possible. But, as a stay against discouragement while mired in a state of uncertainty, consider this: You may, right now, be uncertain about a particular matter, but that experience is only possible because you have known the opposite experience, the experience of being certain about something. (The principle is this: A negative can only be recognized as a negative—"uncertainty"—because its positive opposite is already known.) Therefore you know that certainty is a real possibility. If certainty is possible at all, then it is possible, eventually, with regard to the matter about which you are now uncertain. There is nothing to preclude, theoretically, your one day overcoming the uncertainty about a particular matter you are now experiencing.

3. There's an Explanation for Everything, Eventually

The principle of sufficient reason tells us that things don't just happen. They are caused to happen. We do not know the causes of everything, but we know that everything has a cause. A good part of our energies as rational creatures is devoted to the search for causes. We want to know why things happen. The knowledge of causes, simply from a theoretical point of view, can be very satisfying, since to know the causes of things is to have a truly profound understanding of them. But the knowledge of causes also has wide-ranging practical implications, for in many instances to know causes is to be able to control them, and to control causes is to control effects. If we know a certain bacterium is the cause of a particular disease, we may be in a position to eliminate the disease (effect) by negating the causal activity of the bacterium.

In the search for causes we obviously begin with effects. We are confronted with a phenomenon of one kind or another—an object, a state of affairs, an event—and we are seeking an explanation for it. There is no doubt in our minds that we are dealing with objective facts; our doubts concern only how those facts came to be. Our search is given systematic direction by the principle that there is a certain rudimentary similarity between every cause and its effect. What this means, in terms of the cause, is that it must be capable of bringing about just the kind of effects we are witnessing. And, in doing so, it leaves its peculiar mark on the effect. That being the case, every effect, to some degree or another, reflects the nature of its cause.

What are the practical implications of this? I cannot know directly what a cause is capable of effecting when it is precisely that cause I am looking for, but I can get an indirect knowledge of its causal capability through the effect that is right before me. It is by carefully sizing up the nature of the effect that I can get some understanding of the nature of the cause, and that knowledge will guide me in my search.

Let us say I am working in my study. I hear an odd noise coming from the kitchen. I go to investigate. On the floor lie the contents of a half-gallon bottle of milk that I had carelessly left on the counter. This is an objective matter of fact: the effect. What is the cause? On the counter, I see three ants near the bottle. The ants? No, they would not have been able to bring about an effect of this magnitude. I note that my canary is out of its cage and perched on top of the refrigerator. The canary? Once again, no. The effect is beyond the capacities of the canary. Then, through the open window, I see, out in the backyard, my neighbor's cat. Aha! Though I cannot be positive that the cat was the cause of the spilled milk, I know that a cat would at least be capable of bringing about such an effect. More investigation needs to be done, but at the moment I can at least consider the cat to be a possible cause of the spilled milk. He is under serious suspicion.

4. Don't Stop Short in the Search for Causes

Causes often arrange themselves in a series. For example, let us suppose that we have a situation in which A is the cause of B. Next, we note that B is in turn the cause of C. We end up with a sequence that can be diagrammed as follows:

$$A \rightarrow B \rightarrow C$$

Let us next suppose that C represents a problematical state of affairs that calls for a quick remedy. Knowing that C has been caused by B, we decide to concentrate our attention on B, guided by the principle that the correct way to deal with problems is to get at their causes.

The logic being followed here is commendable as far as it goes, but it does not go far enough. While it is true that B is the immediate cause of C, it is not its ultimate cause. The causal sequence begins with A, and therefore that is the source of the problem C.

B is clearly the immediate cause of C, so if C is problematical, that means there is something problematical about B. But because B is itself an effect, whatever is problematical about it is to be traced to its cause A. The problem with C will not be effectively addressed, then, until the ultimate source of the problem with A is taken care of.

Let's see if we can put that in plain English. Sam notices a foul odor in the kitchen. Investigating, he discovers that a bucket placed in the cabinet under the sink is filled to the brim with reeking water. Once he empties the bucket, the stench is gone. But it gradually returns as the bucket fills up again. Now, Sam could continue to empty the bucket on a regular basis to meet the problem of the bad smell, but we would be disinclined to give him high marks for intelligence were he to remain satisfied with this solution. The only way to solve the problem once and for all is to get at the root of it and fix the leaky pipes that are the explanation for the bucket continuously filling up.

Sometimes our failure to find the root causes of things is attributable to simple laziness. We don't push the investigation far enough. Other times it is impatience which works against us. We are so pressed by the need to "do something" that we settle for quick fixes, stop-gap measures, while the basic problem remains essentially undisturbed.

5. Distinguish Among Causes

Thus far, we have been dealing primarily with what is called the "efficient cause." The efficient cause, to rephrase what was said earlier, is an agent whose activity brings something into existence or that modifies its existence in one way or another. Besides the efficient cause there are the "final cause," the "material cause," and the "formal cause." Not every type of cause can be applied to everything we are attempting to analyze in terms of causality, but the more types of causes we can identify with something, the more comprehensive is our understanding of it.

The final cause, as applied to activity, is the purpose of the activity; as applied to an object, it is the use to which the object can be put. The material cause is the material out of which an object is composed. The formal cause is the identifying nature of a thing, that which makes it precisely what it is.

Let us analyze a birdhouse in terms of the four causes. Its efficient cause is Fred, who made it. Its material cause is pinewood, the metal of nails, screws, and staples, and paint. Its formal cause is the peculiar configuration of its material, which accounts for its being a birdhouse and not a file box or a window planter. Its final cause is to provide shelter and a nesting site for birds.

As already mentioned, not everything can be analyzed in terms of all four causes. A mathematical idea (or any idea) would not have a material cause, because ideas are immaterial. A mathematician comes up with a particular idea; he would be its efficient cause. Its formal cause would be the specific nature of the idea (e.g., it is about concentric circles), and its final cause, let us say, is to contribute to the solution of a long-standing mathematical problem concerning concentricity and circularity.

In efficient causality a distinction can be made between the "principal cause" and the "instrumental cause." We say that a sculptor is the principal cause of a marble statue, because he is the ultimate explanation for its existence. But he is not the only explanation, for he needed tools to make the statue. In an important sense those tools caused the statue, albeit in a subordinate way—as instruments in the hands of the sculptor. The instruments are the means through which a principal efficient cause brings about a certain effect.

Though instrumental causes are subordinate to principal causes, in many cases they are no less necessary. A great cellist absolutely needs his instrument if he is to bring beautiful cello music into being. It is obvious that the dependence of the instrumental cause on the principal cause is absolute. The instrumental cause is passive and cannot initiate the action of which it is capable. A cello cannot play itself. The quality of both principal and instrumental causes have a bearing on the quality of the effect. The best cello ever made will not produce the best music ever heard in the hands of a cellist of limited talent. And the best cellist in the world will be prevented from making the exquisite music he wants to make, and which he is capable of making, if he has to play an inferior instrument.

Though both the principal and instrumental causes are necessary, the principal cause is the more important of the two, something we tend to forget when we put too much stress on the importance of the instrumental cause. It is doubtless necessary to provide the best instruments possible, but not to the neglect of providing the best instrumentalists possible as well. To repeat, the best instruments in incompetent hands don't bring about the best effects. There is also this to consider: A proficient principal cause can do things with even inferior instruments that an incompetent principal cause couldn't do with even the best of instruments.

6. Define Your Terms

The most effective way to avoid vagueness or ambiguity in logical discourse is to define one's terms. We speak of defining terms, but actually what we are defining is the objects to which terms (words) refer. The process of definition, the mechanics of it, is the way we relate a particular object (the object to be defined) to other objects and thereby give it a precise "location." In defining a term or word, we relate it as rigorously as possible to the object to which it refers. There are two immediate practical benefits of carefully defining terms. Our own ideas are clarified, and, as a result, we can more effectively communicate them to others. Terms such as "justice," "beauty," and "wisdom," which tend toward vagueness, are in special need of definition.

The logical definition of terms is a two-step process. Step one: Place the term to be defined in its "proximate genus." Step two: Identify the term's "specific difference."

The proximate genus is that large class of objects in which the object we want to define belongs because it shares a nature with all the other members of that class. Aristotle's classic definition of man is "the rational animal." In that definition, "animal" is the proximate genus: the most immediate class in which "man" belongs. Why? Because man shares an animal nature with the other members of the class. Aristotle did not choose a class such as "living organism," or "physical substance," or "thing," because these would be too broad. The "man" he wanted to define would have been grouped with all sorts of objects with which it did not share a nature.

Consider an assortment of toys in a large toy box placed in a room in a house located in Lansing, Iowa. We could say the toys are in the toy box, or in the room, or in the house, or in Lansing, Iowa. All statements would be true. But the toy box would be comparable to the proximate genus. There are different kinds of toys, but because they are all toys, they belong in the toy box. That is their proper "class."

The specific difference is the characteristic (or characteristics) that sets apart the object we want to define from other objects in its genus. In Aristotle's definition of man, a single characteristic, rationality, is cited as differentiating man from all the other animals. The specific difference literally *specifies;* that is, it identifies a particular species and sets it apart from other species in its genus. When we define something, what we are attempting to do is simply identify it more precisely—first by grouping it with other things that are *generally* similar to it, then by noting what is unique to it (the specific difference) in comparison with the other things in the group.

Let us try it with a couple of challenging terms.

a) Term to be defined: justice.

> Step 1: "Justice is a social virtue . . ."
> Step 2: ". . . by which each individual renders to all others what is due to them."

COMMENT: "Social virtue" is the right category (proximate genus) in which to put our term because it provides an accurate general description of it. Categories like "mineral" or "institution" or "event" would obviously be wrong for the term. Categories such as "something" or "concept" or "phenomenon" would be too large; they would lack the quality of proximity (as in "proximate genus"). But while justice is a social virtue, it is not the only one. What, then, distinguishes it from other social virtues, such as courtesy, generosity, or tolerance? The specific difference we have given in the definition pinpoints its uniqueness, as a social virtue, rather nicely.

b) Term to be defined: fear.

Step 1: "Fear is an emotion . . ."
Step 2: ". . . that causes us to withdraw from per-
ceived danger."

COMMENT: "Sense appetite" is another term that could be used to identify the proximate genus. The specific difference succeeds in telling us precisely what kind of emotion we are dealing with.

Aristotle's pithy two-word definition of man—the rational animal—has gained classical status. "Animal" is the proximate genus; "rational" is the specific difference. But seldom can we match that kind of economy, especially when it comes to specific difference. If we were to define "automobile," for example, taking the first step would be easy enough: "vehicle." But then we would have to come up with several specific differences in order to distinguish it precisely from all the other kinds of vehicles there are in the world.

The special value of logical definition is that it reveals the exact nature of the object defined. Such definition is not always possible, however, as when we are not yet familiar enough with an object to be able to determine its exact nature. In such a case we can define the object in a loose way, by description. A good description gives as complete and detailed an account of the observable characteristics of an object as possible. The hope is that this account will provide some revealing hints as to the nature of the object in question.

7. *The Categorical Statement*

The purpose of the reasoning process, logic's principal concern, is demonstration. I am not reasoning with you if I simply *say* that such-and-such is true and expect you to accept it as true only on my say-so. I must *show* you that such-and-such is true, and I do that by making an argument. An argument will only be as good as the statements of which it is composed, and those statements, in turn, will only be as good as the terms of which they are composed. Everything I have said thus far has been said with argument in mind. Argument is *the* activity of logic, and any particular argument is a concrete manifestation of the reasoning process. The next step in the process will be to look more closely at the statement, more specifically, at the "categorical statement." The most effective argument is one whose conclusion is a categorical statement. A categorical statement tells us that something definitely is the case. For example, "The radio is in the backseat of the car." We are certain as to what is the actual situation here. But if someone says, "Perhaps the radio is in the backseat of the car," or "The radio may be in the backseat of the car," all certitude is gone. Those are not categorical statements, and we are left in doubt as to what actually is the case. A categorical argument (one made up of categorical statements) is the most effective of arguments, then, because it provides us with certain knowledge. But it is the actual situation which determines whether or not we are allowed to speak in categorical statements. For example, if I have genuine doubts as to the whereabouts of the radio, it would be irresponsible of me to state categorically that it is in the back of the car. But whenever the situation warrants it, that is, whenever we have real certitude, we should express that certitude by speaking categorically.

A word of caution. A statement may be categorical in form but may not express what is *objectively* the case. A person may say, "The Chicago Cubs are the best team in baseball." That is a categorical statement, but what it tells us is that the person making it has no doubts about this particular matter. It reveals what is subjectively the case, because it declares what is, in fact, the speaker's opinion. But it does not refer to any objective state of affairs.

8. *Generalizing*

A general statement is one whose subject is very large in scope. Such a statement is not necessarily inaccurate. "Horses are vertebrates" and "Houses are domestic dwellings" are general statements, and there is no reason to dispute the claims they are making. What makes a general statement sound is the fact that what is being attributed to the class represented by the subject is (a) true and (b) in fact applies to the entire class.

In a statement like "Horses are vertebrates," the assumption is that each and every member of the class specified by the subject ("horses") is being referred to. But the language of the statement does not make that explicit. In order to eliminate any doubt about the matter, we add the qualifier "all" to the statement: "All horses are vertebrates." And, if we do not intend to refer to each and every member of the subject class, then we must be explicit in our language: "Some houses are bungalows."

Explicit language in general statements is important because it guards against any possible confusion on the part of an audience. Some people deliberately leave out linguistic qualifiers ("all," "some") because they want what they are saying to be understood as applying to an entire class without being explicit about it. In more cases than not, a statement such as "Carthaginians are cruel and stupid" is meant to refer to *all* Carthaginians. If one who makes such a claim is called to task, he can use as an out the fact that he didn't say *all* Carthaginians are cruel and stupid. True, he didn't say it, but he implied it.

There are two types of general statements, the universal and the particular. A "universal affirmative statement" is an "every" or "all" statement ("All whales are mammals"). It affirms something about an entire class. A "universal negative statement" is a "no" statement ("No fish have feet"). It denies something of an entire class. A "particular statement," affirmative or negative, does not refer to each and every member of the class specified by its subject. It is usually marked by the qualifier "some" ("Some mammals are arboreal"; "Some potatoes are not new"). But the statements "Most adult Americans drive cars" and "The majority of the junior class voted for Peterson" are also particular statements. So long as the *entire* class is not being referred to, the statement is particular. Be it large or small, a portion is a portion.

When we refer to a statement's being universal or particular, we are concerned with what in logical language is called the "quantity" of the statement. The "singular statement" stands in contrast to the "general statement"; it is characterized by the fact that its subject is an individual. "Mary is from Maryland" is a singular statement; so is "Wrigley Field is in Chicago."

"Universal statements," affirmative or negative, are very precise. They are affirming or denying something of an entire class, with no exceptions. Particular statements, on the other hand, are usually rather vague. "Some" covers a lot of territory; it could mean 99 percent or 2 percent. But it is possible for particular statements to be quite precise: "Sixteen percent of the runners finished the race in under two hours." Always be as precise in your statements about things as your knowledge of them allows you to be.

PART THREE

Argument: The Language of Logic

The concrete expression of logical reasoning is the argument. An argument stands or falls to the extent that the reasoning it incorporates is good or bad. In this section, we examine all that goes into the making of a healthy and effective argument.

1. Founding an Argument

The basic move of reasoning, the inferential move, is that by which we go from one idea that is known to be true to a second idea, which is recognized as true on the force of the first idea. This move constitutes the heart of argumentation. Arguments, as we saw, are composed of statements, and it is the statements within an argument that convey the ideas with which the inferential move is concerned.

Arguments can get complicated, chiefly by reason of the number of statements they may contain, but every argument, no matter how complicated, is extremely simple in its essential character. Every argument is composed of two basic elements, two different types of statements: a "premise" statement and a "conclusion" statement. A premise is a supporting statement. It is the starting point of an argument, containing the known truth from which the inferential move begins. A conclusion is a supported statement, the statement that is accepted as true on the basis of the premise. Complicated arguments usually result from the large number of premises they contain, as mentioned, and from how those premises relate to one another. You can have a set of premises in which one builds on another, so they have to be arranged in the proper sequence. For example: "Because the nail came out of the horseshoe, because the horseshoe came off, because the horse grew lame, because the horse fell down and threw the general, because the general was captured, the battle was lost." It is rare to have multiple conclusions to an argument. And, in fact, they are to be avoided. A single conclusion is always best. This is just another way of saying that the most effective arguments are those that are trying to make a single point.

The simplest argument is one composed of two statements, a supporting statement or premise and a supported statement or conclusion. Usually, the context of the argument will allow you to tell which is which, but we attach what are called "logical indicators" to statements in order to mark them clearly as either premises or conclusions. Common logical indicators for premises are "because," "since," "on account of." Common logical indicators for conclusions are "therefore," "thus," "so." More elaborate expressions can be used to announce premises ("in view of the fact that," etc.) and conclusions ("it necessarily follows that," etc.). Consider this simple explanatory argument:

Because he was constantly disputing with his boss,
Dave was transferred to the Houston office.

COMMENT: The argument isn't trying to establish a matter of fact, Dave's transfer, but to explain it, to give the reason why it occurred. The first statement, the premise, is offered as supporting information in that, if we accept it as true, we now understand why the transfer took place.

The premise is the foundation of an argument. The soundness of this foundation depends entirely on the truth of the premise. The first order of business, then, in building a sound argument is to ensure the truth of the premise. In the argument above, if it is not true that Dave was constantly disputing with his boss, then we remain without an explanation for his transfer. Besides the imperative requirement that it be true, a premise, in order to provide a sound foundation for argument, must be sufficiently wide in scope to contain the conclusion. This is a point I will discuss in sections 14 and 15.

2. The Move from Universal to Particular

The nature of a universal statement is such that, if it is true, a particular statement with the same subject and predicate is also true. So, if it is true that every dog is carnivorous, then it is true that some dogs are carnivorous. If no males are mothers is true, then that some males are not mothers is also true. Those are neither very informative nor very interesting conclusions, but the simple inferences that produce them are worth pausing over for a moment, because they provide us with a vivid example of necessitation in argument. Given the truth of the premise that all dogs are carnivorous, there can be no doubt whatsoever about the truth of the conclusion that some dogs are carnivorous. And there is no escaping the truth that some males are not mothers, once we recognize that no males are mothers. Those conclusions, as we say, follow necessarily. A "necessary conclusion" is one that it is not possible to doubt—it is certain.

The logic behind the move from universal to particular, and the necessity it entails, is simple enough. If I know something to be true about an entire group, then it must also be true about any portion of the group.

3. The Move from Particular to Universal

The move from universal to particular ensures a necessarily true conclusion. The movement from particular to universal offers no such assurance. Knowledge of a part does not allow me to say anything definitive about the whole. In some instances, any attempt to make that move would yield a conclusion that is manifestly false. "Some women are mothers" is a statement about whose truth I can be perfectly confident. But I am not allowed to use it to support the conclusion that every woman is a mother. This shows us that it is not enough for a premise be true to make it a sound foundation for an argument. It must also be sufficiently large in scope to encompass the conclusion, and that's precisely what cannot happen if the premise is a particular statement and the conclusion a universal statement. The whole can contain a part, but a part cannot contain the whole.

Is there any legitimate way we can move from particular to universal? Yes, so long as we take care not to claim anything beyond what the evidence allows us to claim. We cannot put forward certain conclusions, but we can suggest probable ones. The move here, in other words, must be a cautious one. If every citizen of County Clare I've met to date—and let's say it's a goodly number—has had red hair and green eyes, it would not be completely irresponsible of me to say something like, "It may be the case that all citizens of County Clare have red hair and green eyes." Whether my conjecture is a likely one is another story.

It is a pretty obvious mistake to claim that something is necessarily true for a whole group because it happens to be true for a part of the group. But that mistake has to have special attention called to it because, for all its obviousness, it is one we are constantly falling into. It easily qualifies as one of the human family's favorite fallacies.

4. Predication

A statement, we recall, is a linguistic expression which makes an assertion that can be affirmed or denied. Grammatically considered, every statement is composed of a subject and a predicate. That about which something is said is the subject; what is said is the predicate. "Predication," then, is the idea-connecting process by which we attribute something to something else. "Loraine is the assistant conductor." In that statement the idea of being the assistant conductor is predicated of Loraine.

If predication is the process of bringing ideas together and coupling them, then the test of sound predication is that the ideas that are brought together belong together. Ideas belong together if their grammatical connection reflects a real connection in the objective order of things. In the statement "Measles is infectious," infectiousness is predicated of measles. This is a sound predication because the subject and predicate do indeed belong together. The statement reflects a real connection. The same can be said for the statement "Ulysses S. Grant was born in Ohio." Being born in Ohio is properly predicated of Grant because the statement reflects what is actually the case.

It can be seen, then, that the upshot of sound predication is that we end up with true statements. Conversely, unsound predication results in false statements. "Jane Austen wrote *Persuasion* in New Hampshire" is false because writing *Persuasion* in New Hampshire cannot be predicated of Jane Austen.

5. *Negative Statements*

"Affirmative statements" connect ideas; "negative statements" disconnect ideas. A "universal negative statement" disconnects ideas completely ("No philosophers are infallible"); a "particular negative statement" disconnects ideas incompletely ("Some North Dakotans do not read Dickens").

When we say that a statement can be affirmed or denied, we are saying merely that it can be true or false. The denial of a statement, then, simply means to declare it to be false. A statement can be false irrespective of its being affirmative or negative. (When we speak, in logical language, of the "quality" of a statement, we are referring to its being either affirmative or negative.) "Herman Melville was never president of the United States" is true; "*Moby-Dick* is not about a whale" is false.

Negative statements can sometimes be tricky, and we must be careful, when we use them, to make sure they are actually saying what we intend them to say. Consider the statement "All dogs are not mongrels." We note the "all," a sign of universality, and the negative indicator "not," and we might be tempted too quickly to suppose that what we have here is a universal negative statement. In fact, it is a particular negative statement. In a universal negative statement a complete severance is made between subject and predicate, but that is not what is happening in this construction. The key to the negative message of the statement can be expressed in the phrase "not all." "Not all" (or "not every") does not mean the same thing as "none"; it translates as "some." The predicate of the statement ("mongrels") is not being separated from the entire class represented by the subject ("dog") but from only a part of it. What the statement is saying, then, is "Some dogs are not mongrels."

All things being equal, if the same idea can be communicated both affirmatively and negatively, it is better to opt for the affirmative construction. Consider the two statements "Some of the students are hard workers" and "Some of the students are not hard workers." From a strictly logical point of view, the two statements are doing the same thing—establishing a partial separation between subject and predicate. But there is a subtle difference between the two statements. The affirmative statement is more direct and emphatic. (This is true of all affirmative statements.) Because its emphasis is on what *is* the case rather than on what is *not* the case, it elicits a positive response. The negative statement, by emphasizing what is not the case, prompts us to think in negative terms about the situation being described.

Negative statements can be effectively used as corrective responses to false statements. "Not every artist is a neurotic" and "Every artist is *not* a neurotic" both are proper rejoinders to the sweeping assertion "Every artist is a neurotic." In logical discourse clarity must always be the foremost consideration, but we create the possibility for confusion when we incorporate negative elements into a statement intended to communicate an affirmative message. "It is not unfair to impose the fine" means the same as "It is fair to impose the fine," but that meaning is conveyed more clearly and directly in the second statement than in the first.

But we do not want to be so rigid in our logical considerations of language that we deny a place for circumlocution that makes use of negation. "It was an idiotic decision" is a clear statement, but also a bit too blunt. More might be gained for the cause of amicable human relations by saying, "The decision was perhaps not the most prudent that could have been made at the time." But one should be reluctant to lay down rigid rules here. Circumstances should dictate the degree of forthrightness in the language we use. Blunt language need not be peremptorily precluded, since certain circumstances call for it.

6. Making Comparisons

The human mind thrives on comparison. Indeed, thought would be impossible without it. It is through the mental act of comparison that we note the similarities and dissimilarities among things.

A "statement" is the linguistic expression of the most fundamental comparison the mind makes when it relates one idea (the subject) to another (the predicate). We call "judgment" the mental act by which we link ideas in a way that enables us to make coherent statements about the world in which we live. Because the judgment is the foundation for the statement, what we have already said about statements applies, by necessity, to judgments. A judgment is sound to the extent that the relationship it forges between two ideas reflects a real relationship in the objective world.

The comparison reflected in the statement is foundational, in that it is the source for the whole complex array of other comparisons we make between and among statements which together constitute the content of our thought. If we were not able to see connections between and among things as a result of the act of comparison, our thought would be completely incoherent. We might have ideas, but each idea would be an isolated entity. We would not see how idea connects with idea to reflect the connections that obtain among objects external to the mind.

When we look at two things for the purpose of comparing them, we can discover that they are either completely alike, completely unlike, or a combination of likeness and unlikeness. (Of course, we can make comparisons among an indefinite number of things, but to keep it simple I speak of two things only.) What would be the basis for the conclusion that the two things we are comparing are completely alike? It would be the fact that every observable characteristic we note in the first thing is matched by a similar characteristic in the second. Consider, for example, comparing two mass-produced coffeemakers, straight from the factory, that are identical in every detail.

The "somewhat alike, somewhat unlike" judgment is almost never perfectly balanced between similar and dissimilar features. The similar features either outweigh the dissimilar, or vice versa. But, whatever the particulars, here too the judgment as such is based upon a careful accounting of observable characteristics.

How about the judgment that two things are totally unlike? How is it justified? It would seem, if the "completely alike" judgment is justified by the fact that the two things being compared have every observable feature in common, that the "totally unlike" judgment would be justified by the fact that the two things being compared have no observable features in common. But is that ever the case? Let us say that, instead of comparing two standardized coffeemakers, we are comparing a coffeemaker and a toaster. Obviously, they differ in many ways. But they can also be observed to have real similarities. To begin with, they are both electrical appliances. Furthermore, they may both be the same color, or weigh the same, or both may be made, for the most part, of the same materials.

(Note this about the "completely alike" judgment: No two things can be so alike that they cease to be two things. If two things were to be identical in the literal sense, there would be but one thing.

Note this about the "completely unlike" judgment: No two things can be so unlike that they do not share the elemental act of existence. If, in comparing A and B, it is declared that B is "totally unlike" A, then there would be but one thing, A, since B would not exist.)

In comparing any two things, especially large, complex things such as historical events, we must be careful not to rush to the judgment that we have a strong comparison ("the two events are very much alike") simply because of the large number of similar characteristics we have noted. It should not be the sheer number of similar characteristics that decides the issue, but the *significance* of those characteristics. A characteristic is significant if it reveals something that pertains to the very nature of the thing. It speaks to the thing's proper identity.

Even a goodly number of similar significant characteristics does not make a strong comparison if a key significant characteristic is omitted. Let us say I am addressing an audience that knows nothing at all about either mice or elephants. In my earnest desire to enlighten the audience, I make a comparison of the two animals. I tell them that both mice and elephants have four feet, two eyes, two ears, a mouth, a tongue, a tail, a heart, and so on. All are significant characteristics. But in my account I make no mention of the comparative size of the animals. I would have left out a rather important significant characteristic.

7. Comparison and Argument

When we bring argument to bear on comparison, our purpose is to demonstrate (i.e., prove by argument) that the two things we are comparing are in fact similar. Let us say I am comparing two things, A and B. I study both of them closely. I make a careful list of the characteristics they have in common. In constructing an argument, my conclusion will be: "A and B are very much alike." The premises of my argument would be the list of common characteristics that I have observed: "Because A and B share trait X, Because A and B share trait Y," and so on. For example, I could be concerned with comparing deer and domestic cattle, and I say that because both deer and cattle have cloven hooves, because both deer and cattle are vegetarian, etc. If, apropos of what was discussed above, I ensure that (1) all the characteristics I cite are significant, and (2) I do not leave out any significant characteristics, my argument is sound and stands a good chance of being persuasive. In this argument I would be heading toward a conclusion that claims a significant similarity between deer and cattle.

One of the most common arguments based on comparison is called "the argument by analogy." (An analogy is a relation of similarity between two things.) The basic structure of the argument is this: Of two things I am comparing, one of them, A, is better known to you than B. The aim of my argument is to persuade you that A and B have enough obvious undisputed points in common that an additional point, which is not so obvious and therefore disputable, is also shared by them. Let A stand for a historical event, such as the Vietnam War, and B for a future course of action the United States government is now contemplating—let's call it Operation Pure Altruism. My task is to convince you that there are enough similarities between the Vietnam War and Operation Pure Altruism that if the government were in fact to embark upon the latter, the experience would be comparable to that of the Vietnam War.

> Outline of argument:
> A possesses traits R, S, T, U, V, W, X, and Y,
> B possesses traits R, S, T, U, V, W, X, and Y,
> A possesses trait Z,
> Therefore B also possesses trait Z.

COMMENT: The conclusion does not follow necessarily, but it is not improbable. Given the fact that two things have many characteristics in common, it seems possible that an additional characteristic, known to be possessed by one thing, would be possessed by the other as well. An argument of this type is employed only in those circumstances in which one cannot *directly* determine whether or not B has trait Z, which of course would be the case if B were an event that has not yet happened and therefore cannot be analyzed.

8. Sound Argument

An argument, as we have seen, has two basic elements: premises and a conclusion. If an economist makes a statement—for instance, that inflation will diminish sharply within the next six months—and expects it to be accepted as true without offering any further information about the matter, the worth of the statement rests upon the economist's authority alone. It is not irresponsible to accept statements as true solely on the authority of those who pronounce them. We do it all the time. If someone is a genuine expert, we can reasonably expect that what he says, so long as he keeps within his area of expertise, is worth listening to. But the kind of knowledge that an argument can provide us is more sure than that based upon voices of authority. This is because when we have assimilated a sound argument, we have in effect seen for ourselves that something is true. We know the "whys" behind our knowledge.

In order for an argument to be sound, it must be so with respect to its matter (its contents) and to its form (its structure). We have already given some attention to the first requirement. An argument is sound with respect to its matter if all the statements it is composed of are true. The importance of that criterion is obvious enough; the second requirement relates to the validity of an argument. An argument is valid if its structure is sound, which means that its structure is such that true premises will ensure a true conclusion. The nature of validity is not always rendered perfectly clear on the force of a verbal description of it, so if the one just given did not turn on the lights for you, be patient. Later, when discussing the structure of argument, to which validity is directly related, I will illustrate validity through examples.

It is important to be aware of the difference between truth and validity. Though often confused, they are in fact quite different. First, truth has to do only with statements, whereas validity has to do only with that structural arrangement of statements that we call an argument. Second, a statement is true if what it asserts reflects what is objectively the case. An argument is valid, to echo what was just said, if its structure is such that it will ensure a true conclusion—if its premises are true.

We have already dealt with a simple form of argument in our discussion of the move from universal to particular statements. We will now look at various other forms of simple arguments by way of leading up to our treatment of the syllogism, the argument that represents the most finished form of reasoning. Here are the three forms of argument we will discuss: "conjunctive," "disjunctive," and "conditional."

CONJUNCTIVE ARGUMENT

The form of the conjunctive argument, expressed symbolically, is A · B. Both A and B represent complete statements. An example in plain English: "Anne is a sophomore at the University of Minnesota and she is majoring in biology." That innocent little "·" tucked between the A and the B, which translates as "and," bears great meaning. It tells us that *both* A and B are true. This is a package deal; you can't isolate one term and take that as true while regarding the other as false. A · B can serve as a premise for an argument, and two conclusions can validly follow from it. Thus:

A · B   A · B
Therefore, A   Therefore, B

COMMENT: Both -A and -B (denying that Anne is really a sophomore at the University of Minnesota or that she is really majoring in biology) are false because they contradict what is stated in the argument's premise.

DISJUNCTIVE ARGUMENT

The disjunctive argument is represented symbolically as follows: A v B. Once again, A and B stand for complete statements. The symbol "v" stands for "or." Example: "Arden either took the train to Washington last night or he took a plane there." Here we are dealing with a strict or "exclusive disjunctive" statement. That means that the two components of the statement are mutually exclusive. They both cannot be true. If one is true, the other must be false, and vice versa. Also—and this is important—both of the components cannot be false. If they were, that would render the expression deceptive, for if we say "either A or B," we are saying that one or the other is the case. If we mean "neither A nor B," then that is what we must say. The valid disjunctive arguments are as follows:

A v B	A v B	A v B	A v B
A	B	-A	-B
Therefore, -B	Therefore, -A	Therefore, B	Therefore, A

COMMENT: In the above notation, -A means "not A" and -B means "not B." Observe that in these arguments an additional step has been added in comparison to the conjunctive argument. In the first example above, instead of moving directly from the initial statement (A v B) to the conclusion (therefore -B), here we need an intervening statement, A, to complete the argument. Specifically, we have to be informed which of the two disjunctions (A, B) is true. In this argument, then, we have two premises: A v B is the major premise; A is the minor premise.

The logic of the above arguments is as follows: Because A and B are mutually exclusive, if one is true the other is false, and vice versa. And A and B are the only two possibilities. So if I know for sure that Arden took the train to Washington, he cannot have taken a plane; if I know for sure he took a plane, he cannot have taken the train. Conversely, if I know for sure he did not take the train, he must have taken a plane; if I know for sure he did not take a plane, he must have taken the train. There are only two possibilities.

9. *Conditional Argument*

Conditional argument, sometimes called "hypothetical" argument, is an "if/then" argument. It reflects a way we habitually think. For instance, "If the weather is nice on Thursday, we'll go on a picnic." Or, "If you work hard, you will eventually attain your goal." A certain condition is set with the idea in mind that, if that condition is met, then certain consequences will follow. Let's take a closer look at this important kind of argument in symbolic form.

$A \rightarrow B$

A

Therefore, B

We begin with the conditional statement A → B. (If A, then B.) A conditional statement, like a conjunctive and a disjunctive statement, is really a compound statement. In other words, in this case A is a statement ("If the Bulldogs win the game") and B is a statement ("They will go to the playoffs"). The first statement is called the "antecedent"; the second is called the "consequent." "A → B" (the first line) is the major premise of the argument; "A" (the second line) is the minor premise. The third line, "Therefore, B," is obviously the argument's conclusion. (The word "therefore" is, again, the logical indicator that identifies the statement as a conclusion.)

The gist of the argument is that the major premise, A → B, tells us that if A (whatever it is) comes about, B will necessarily follow. At this point we do not know what will or will not actually happen. The minor premise, A, tells us that the condition established in the major premise has been fulfilled. That being the case, then the consequent, B, will come about. This is a valid argument, meaning that if the premises are true, the conclusion will also necessarily be true. That is the guarantee of a valid argument: True premises yield a true conclusion.

But in order to appreciate the validity of conditional argument, we must have a very clear understanding of what precisely the major premise, A → B, is telling us. It is saying that the link between A and B is absolutely necessary. In other words, If A comes about, then B *must* come about.

This being the case, it should be apparent that most of the conditional arguments we use in our daily lives are not such in the strict logical sense. Consider an earlier example:

"If the weather is nice on Thursday, we'll go on a picnic." If we reflect on that statement, we will see that there is no necessary connection between the antecedent (nice weather on Thursday) and the consequent (going on a picnic). The weather could be ideal on Thursday and yet, for any number of reasons not now foreseen, there may be no picnic. But consider this argument:

> If Louise is running, then Louise is moving.
> But Louise is in fact running.
> Therefore, Louise is moving.

Here we can see that there is a strict bond of necessity between antecedent and consequent. There is no way in the world Louise could be running and yet not moving at the same time, so the argument's conclusion is necessarily true.

There is another valid form of conditional argument, symbolically schematized as follows:

> A → B
> -B
> Therefore, -A

The major premise sets the condition: "If Louise is running, then she is moving." The minor premise (-B) tells us: "Louise is not moving." Conclusion: "Therefore, she is not running." The logic of the argument: Because running necessarily entails moving (since it is impossible to be running and not moving), if one is not moving, then obviously one cannot be running. (In Part Five, sections 1 and 2, where I discuss fallacious reasoning, I will take up the invalid forms of conditional argument.)

Though we depend heavily on the kind of reasoning exemplified by conditional argument, it is rare, again, that we use it in the strict logical sense. Seldom is it the case that there is a real necessary connection between antecedent and consequent in our arguments. The result of this is that the conclusions we reach in our arguments do not necessarily follow. This does not mean, however, that conditional argument that yields anything less than necessary conclusions is of no value, much less that it is irresponsible to use such argument. In the vast majority of conditional arguments we use, our conclusions will be probable ones. Our aim should be to construct our arguments in such a way that their conclusions will carry as high a degree of probability as possible.

Imagine that a friend says to you, "If I win the lottery, I will donate all those millions to charity." Hearing that, you very likely would not be expecting your friend's favorite charities to be soon rolling in money. Your skepticism would be based on the fact that a very big "if" has been laid down by the statement; the chances of the condition being met are minuscule. And suppose that condition should be met. Does that mean that your friend would necessarily give his new-found wealth to charity?

In a conditional argument that does not entail necessity, the stronger the connection between antecedent and consequent, the more probable it is that the consequent will turn out to be true. Let me return to an example I used earlier: "If the Bulldogs win the game, they will be in the playoffs." Let's assume that this describes a situation based on objective fact. Given their present record, if they win the game, the Bulldogs are guaranteed a spot in the playoffs. However, the connection between antecedent (winning the game) and consequent (getting in the playoffs) is not a necessary one. The Bulldogs could win the game and, let us say, there could be a players' strike, canceling the playoffs for this year. But in fact a strike seems unlikely, so, all things considered, the bond between antecedent and consequent is quite strong. It would not be imprudent betting on the Bulldogs to make the playoffs assuming they will win the game.

The strength of your conditional argument depends on your knowledge of the two things you are bringing together in the conditional statement that leads off the argument, and of how they are related. If the relation between antecedent and consequent is tenuous, it would be rash to argue as if it were otherwise. Notice that conditional argument is future-oriented, and therefore potentially predictive. Reliable predictions are based upon a knowledge of the patterns of the past. "If Uncle Louis comes to town," you say, "he's going to want to go to Schmidty's for supper." That is a reasonable prediction because you know that every year for the past fifteen when Uncle Louis has come to town he's invariably wanted to go to Schmidty's for supper.

10. Syllogistic Argument

The syllogism is a form of argument that reflects the way the human mind habitually operates: that is, connecting ideas in such a way that conclusions can be drawn from those connections. Let us begin our discussion of this form of argument, as we did with the simpler forms, by acquainting ourselves with its structure and identifying its various parts. Here is a syllogistic argument in partially symbolic form:

> Every M is P
> Every S is M
> Therefore, every S is P

The first statement is the major premise; the second is the minor premise. The third is clearly recognizable as the conclusion. The three letters, M, P, S, represent the terms of which the three statements are composed—the ideas as expressed in words. M represents the "middle term," P the "major term," and S the "minor term." The middle term is particularly important, since its task is to forge a link between the other two terms, and the success of the argument depends on its ability to do so. Here is an example of the argument in plain English:

> Every NFL player is a professional athlete.
> The Minnesota Vikings are NFL players.
> Thus, the Minnesota Vikings are professional athletes.

One does not need to know what "NFL" stands for or who the Minnesota Vikings are to be able to see, by its structure alone, that this argument makes sense.

Syllogistic reasoning is based upon the operation of relating a part to a whole in order to establish clearly something about the part. If A is a part of a whole, B, then it shares, as a part, what is common to the whole.

The major premise of our argument (every M is P) can be illustrated as follows:

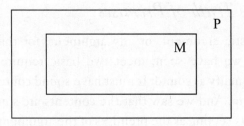

Note that M, representing the smaller group, is completely incorporated within the larger group, P. Next we can illustrate the minor premise (every S is M) thus:

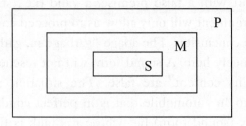

The minor premise repeats the operation of the major premise; that is, it incorporates a smaller group into a larger one. Now, with these two operations completed, the three terms of the argument have been connected and we can literally see how the conclusion indeed follows. There is no avoiding it. If M is a part of P, and if S is a part of M, then S must be a part of P as well.

11. The Truth of Premises

A syllogistic argument, or any argument, for that matter, must, as we have seen, meet two basic requirements in order to qualify as sound: It must have sound contents and a sound form. And we saw that the contents are sound if the statements serving as the premises of the argument are true. Look at what we end up with if we have an argument that is structurally sound but whose contents are unsound:

> Every dog has three heads.
> Collies are dogs.
> Therefore, collies have three heads.

If we start with a false premise, a valid (i.e., structurally sound) argument will only allow us to proceed consistently to a false conclusion. The adage "garbage in, garbage out" applies nicely here. A sound form will not rescue an argument if its contents are false. The situation might be likened to an automobile that is in perfect condition mechanically (sound form) but whose gas tank is filled with water (unsound contents). The best of vehicles will not get us to where we want to go without the gas. Validity is not enough.

12. The Relevancy of Premises

While the truth of the premises is a necessary condition for sound argument, it is not a sufficient condition. True premises may not contribute much to the argument if they poorly support its conclusion. Recall that the purpose of premises is to support a conclusion, to give us some persuasive reasons for accepting it; but if premises, though true, are weak, they cannot do this. One of the ways premises display weakness is by not being to the point of the conclusion. Consider this example:

> Pierre Poseur was an All-American football player.
> Pierre Poseur earned his first million before he was thirty.
> Pierre Poseur is handsome and has a winning smile.
> Therefore, Pierre Poseur should be elected governor.

Let us assume that everything said of Mr. Poseur in the premises is true. He was in fact an All-American, he did earn his first million before he was thirty, and he is a handsome devil with a winning smile. But all of this, though true, is not really relevant to the issue at hand. It tells us nothing about what specific qualifications he might have which would enable him to assume the weighty responsibilities associated with being governor of the state.

Now consider another argument, this one in favor of his opponent:

> John Vere spent four years in the Peace Corps.
> He is a constitutional lawyer.
> He was mayor of Center City for two terms.
> He has served in the state legislature for twelve years.
> Therefore, he should be elected governor.

The premises of this argument have a more direct relationship to the conclusion than do the premises of the previous argument. We may not be compelled by them, but we would be reluctant to dismiss them as having no bearing on the conclusion.

13. Statements of Fact, Statements of Value

"Musicians are people who make music" is a factual statement. Using such a statement as our starting point, we can make an argument that is sound, if not terribly interesting:

> Musicians are people who make music.
> Dorothy is a musician.
> It follows that Dorothy makes music.

Now consider this statement: "Musicians are superior people." This is a statement not of fact but of value. It expresses the opinion of the one who makes it. There is nothing to prohibit us from making arguments that take off from statements of value. Thus:

> Musicians are superior people.
> Cecilia is a musician.
> Cecilia, therefore, is a superior person.

But what kind of credence are we to give to arguments based upon statements of value, such as in the example above? Not much, I think we would all agree. Note the vagueness of the term "superior." What is that supposed to mean? An argument based upon a statement of value can never have the same kind of conclusiveness as an argument based upon a statement of fact, for evaluations can be contested interminably. But not all statements of value are lacking in soundness. The test for the soundness of a statement of value is the extent to which it is founded upon objective fact. The broader and more solid the foundation of objective fact, the more reliable the statement of value based on it. For example, the evaluative judgments of someone who has a great deal of knowledge in a given area are to be respected, provided of course that those judgments pertain to the area of expertise in question. The evaluative judgments of a Robert Frost on the subject of poetry would carry weight, as would those of a Ted Williams on the subject of baseball, but we would hesitate to put much stock in Frost on baseball or Williams on poetry.

14. Argumentative Form

We have seen that it is possible to have an argument that is not defective in form but that produces false conclusions because its premises are false. In this case, the form is sound, the contents are not. Conversely, it is possible to have an argument whose premises are perfectly true but whose conclusion is false, and this is because the argument's form is defective. Consider the following argument:

> Every squirrel is a mammal.
> Every chipmunk is a mammal.
> Therefore, every chipmunk is a squirrel.

Both the major and minor premises of the argument are true, yet the conclusion is blatantly false. What allows a situation of this kind is invalidity. In this case, the argument's structure is defective. The immediate effect of an invalid (structurally defective) argument is that it prevents the argument's terms from being connected in a way that will bring about a necessarily true conclusion. Let's take another look at the configuration of a valid syllogistic argument, this time expressed only in symbols, so that we can get the clearest sense of how it is put together:

$$\frac{\begin{array}{c} M—P \\ S—M \end{array}}{S—P}$$

The letters, we know, represent the terms of the argument (notice that there are only three, a very important fact). The dashes between the letters represent the verbal connectors ("is," "are"). The line between the second and third statement represents "therefore." You will recall that M represents the middle term. The middle term is simply the one that appears in the premises but not in the conclusion. That is important, for the specific task of the middle term is to connect the other terms, the minor and the major. Note the position of the middle term in the premises. It is the subject term of the major premise and the predicate term of the minor premise. That positioning allows the necessary connection to be made between the major term and the minor term. Now consider a symbolic representation of the argument cited above about squirrels and chipmunks:

$$\frac{\begin{array}{c} P—M \\ S—M \end{array}}{S—P}$$

We can readily see that in this argumentative structure the middle term ("mammal") is the predicate term in both the major premise and the minor premise. That is what renders the argument invalid; this is a defective structure. But why should it be so? To understand the nature of the problem here, we need to keep in mind that the task of the middle term is to connect the major and the minor terms. But this structural arrangement does not allow the middle term to fulfill its task. The specific reason for this has to do with the nature of the predicates of affirmative statements, a matter that now needs to be addressed.

The two statements that serve as the premises in the argument are affirmative, and in both instances the middle term is the predicate. This is what is significant about the predicate terms of affirmative statements: They are always particular (or "undistributed") and never universal (or "distributed"). In the statement "Every squirrel is a mammal," the subject term is universal; the "every" clearly announces that. Yet the predicate term does not refer to all mammals, but only to those that are squirrels. This can be shown if we assume the predicate term to be universal and then reverse the subject and the predicate term. Thus, "Every mammal is a squirrel." This is clearly false.

So, then, we have a situation where the middle term in the argument is a particular or undistributed term in both its appearances, but—and here's the point—the middle term *must be universal at least once* to enable it to make the connection that must be made between minor term and major term in order to yield a conclusion that is not *simply* true but *necessarily* true. An argumentative structure that blocks off the middle term from universality is therefore invalid. The specific name assigned to this problem is "undistributed middle term."

Let us now apply the above analysis to the problematic argument we are discussing. What the premises of the argument do is place two separate subgroups (squirrels and chipmunks) within the same larger group (mammals). The conclusion then attempts to identify the two subgroups because they are both in the same larger group. But common sense tells us that two things can belong to the same general class and yet themselves be in no way the same. A cap can be wool, and so can a sweater, but that does not lead us to confuse a cap with a sweater.

The optimal form for an argument is one that, given true premises, will guarantee a necessarily true conclusion. Such a form is a valid form. The form of the argument we are discussing is invalid because it can offer no such guarantee. But does that mean that an argument with this kind of form should never be used? No. You can structure a responsible argument along these lines if you keep clearly in mind that the conclusion the argument yields can only be probable; it can never be necessary. The strength of the conclusion's probability will depend on the strength of the connections established in the premises. Consider the following argument:

> Halverson was at the Chicago conference in April.
> Policinski was at the same conference.
> It is possible they could have met there.

Note the tentativeness of the conclusion, which is quite appropriate. We cannot say for sure that Halverson and Policinski met at the conference (since all we know is that they were both there), but it is not unreasonable to suppose that they might have encountered each other in the Windy City.

15. *Conclusions Must Reflect Quantity of Premises*

As noted earlier, the "quantity" of a statement refers to its being either universal or particular. The quantity of a statement is established by the quantity of its subject term. "Every pigeon is a bird" is a universal statement. "Some trees are deciduous" is a particular statement. In a syllogistic argument, if there is a particular statement in the premises, it must be reflected in the conclusion. If one of the premises begins with "some," the conclusion must begin with "some."

But quantity must be reflected in the conclusion in a more absolute way. That is, the quantity of a term which appears in the conclusion, be the term a subject or predicate, must not exceed the quantity of that same term as it appears in the premises. In other words, if the term is universal in the conclusion, it must be universal in the premises. In order to make this point clear, let us consider the following argument:

> Every chemist is a scientist.
> Every chemist is hardworking.
> Therefore, every hardworking person is a scientist.

COMMENT: Even if we were to assume both premises to be true, we still intuitively sense that there is something seriously wrong with this argument, but we may not be able immediately to put our finger on just what it is. However, if we look at it closely, keeping in mind something we learned earlier, we can precisely locate the source of the problem. Note that the conclusion makes a claim about "every hardworking person." The term is clearly universal. But if we look at that same term in the minor premise, we see that it is the predicate term of an affirmative proposition, which, we recall from section 14, is always particular in extension, or undistributed. Now, it is illegitimate to move from a term that is particular in the premises and universal in the conclusion, which is what is being done here.

We have said that we can have a particular conclusion only if we have a particular premise. What would happen if we had two particular premises? Let us put the matter to the test in the following argument:

> Some teenagers study Spanish.
> Some chess champions are teenagers.
> Therefore, some chess champions study Spanish.

COMMENT: The conclusion does not follow. It *may* be that some chess players study Spanish; indeed, it is highly probable that some do. But the argument does not prove that this is *necessarily* the case. The general rule that can be stated to explain this is: No conclusion follows from two particular premises. But let's look at the argument more closely to find out why this should be so. What effect on an argument is brought about by two particular premises? Note that the middle term in the argument is "teenagers." It is clearly a particular term in the major premise, "some teenagers."

But, as the predicate term in the minor premise, it is particular there as well. Thus we have a middle term that is not distributed at least once, and therefore it lacks the capacity to make a connection between the major term and the minor term. To see this more clearly, we will first cast the argument in partially symbolic terms:

> Some M are P.
> Some S are M.
> Therefore, Some S are P.

Now let us illustrate the argument with a diagram:

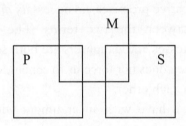

We can see that P can be connected with M, and S be connected with M, without there being any necessary connection between P and S, which the conclusion wrongly assumes there is.

16. Conclusions Must Reflect Quality of Premises

The quality of a statement, remember, refers to its being either affirmative or negative. If the statement that serves as the conclusion of an argument is negative, at least one of the premises in the argument must be negative. Let us see what happens if both of the premises of an argument are negative.

> No men are daughters.
> No waitresses are men.
> Therefore, no waitresses are daughters.

The conclusion is manifestly false. The effect of two negative premises is comparable to that of an undistributed middle term. With an undistributed middle term, no necessary connection is made between minor and major terms. In the case of two negative premises, no necessary *dis*connection is established between the two terms. The fact that the groups of waitresses and daughters are both separated from the group of men does not force us to conclude that they are separated from each other.

What do we have with an argument with affirmative premises followed by a negative conclusion? Consider this one, for example:

> Every bird is a vertebrate.
> Chickadees are birds.
> Therefore, chickadees are not vertebrates.

We have an argument that makes no sense whatever. The conclusion is totally gratuitous, tacked on, as it were, and not in any way based upon the preceding premises. Not to mention quite false.

Now let's look at an argument with a negative conclusion that is true because the argument it terminates is sound.

> No Pennsylvanians are Californians.
> Every Scrantonian is a Pennsylvanian.
> Therefore, no Scrantonians are Californians.

The group of Pennsylvanians is completely separated from the group of Californians (major premise). The subgroup of Scrantonians is completely enclosed within the group of Pennsylvanians (minor premise). That being the case, the subgroup Scrantonians would have to be completely separated from the group of Californians, which is the logical conclusion to the argument.

17. Inductive Argument

All the arguments discussed thus far have been deductive. The conventional way of distinguishing between deductive argument and inductive argument is to say that the former starts from the general and proceeds to the particular, while the latter starts from the particular and proceeds to the general. This is an adequate account of the difference between the two, but a limited one. A more precise way to distinguish them is to say that deductive argument is productive of necessary conclusions, while inductive argument has the capacity to produce probable conclusions only.

Both deduction and induction, as argumentative forms, possess the two elements basic to all argument: premises and a conclusion. In the case of deduction, there is a single starting point (the major premise) that is assumed to be an established fact. It is always a general statement, which means that it refers to a number of things ("Every tree has a root system"). The basic rationale behind deductive reasoning is this: Starting from a statement we know to be true (major premise), we draw out of it and make explicit (through minor premise to conclusion) what is implied in that initial true statement. And that is what's happening in an argument such as this one:

> Every tree has a root system.
> The cottonwood next door is a tree.
> Therefore, the cottonwood next door has a root system.

The truth of the conclusion was already contained in the major premise. The argument brings it out into the open. We could say that deductive argument is analytic because it breaks a general truth down into its constituent parts.

The premises of inductive argument are all the particular facts that go together to serve as a collection of evidence. Those facts provide the basis for making a reliable generalization about them. But what makes researchers start collecting facts of a particular kind in the first place? We say they are guided in their research by hypotheses. A hypothesis is an educated guess as to how things must be, or, at least, how they very likely might be. The formulation of a hypothesis might come as a result of casual observation, prompted by something you just happen to stumble upon, or it could be the result of calculated reasoning.

As a simple example of induction, let us imagine a man,

Harry, living in the dim, distant past, who was very fond of dogs. He had five of them. One day he was visited by his sister and her two young daughters. The two girls, new to the house, were very excited about the dogs and wanted to get acquainted with them. Harry took them into the yard and called over his golden retriever. One niece raised her hand and lowered it over the head of the dog to pet it; the animal started and shied away. The second niece brought her open hand up from below, under the muzzle of the dog, who smelled the hand, then allowed the girl to pat it on the head. "Hm," thought Harry, "very interesting. Was that just a coincidence?"

He asked his nieces if they would be willing to participate in a little experiment. They said they would love to. Harry told them that he was going to call over each of the other four dogs one by one. As each dog was presented, each of the girls was first to lower her hand over the head of the dog, as if to pet it. Next, she was to bring her open hand up under the muzzle of the dog. In each case the dogs shied away from the first gesture, but were receptive and friendly to the second. From that primitive bit of induction, Harry reached the tentative conclusion that dogs generally tend to behave in just those ways under those circumstances.

The whole scientific enterprise rests squarely upon inductive reasoning. Scientists are continually gathering up specific bits of data to see what larger patterns can be discerned from them. Once the patterns are detected, once a regularity of repetitiousness in the patterns is recorded, then reliable prediction is made possible. If I have never known an instance of phenomenon X to have occurred in the past without phenomenon Y also occurring (and I have, let us say, observed hundreds of instances of phenomenon X), then I can reasonably predict that, should phenomenon X occur tomorrow, so will phenomenon Y. Inductive argument thus becomes the basis for deductive argument.

Inductive reasoning is ordered to making reliable generalizations (i.e., those having a high degree of probability) about large groups of things. If it were possible, in the effort to determine whether all the members of a particular group have a particular characteristic, to check out each and every member of the group, then the conclusion one comes up with would be definitive. But this is almost never possible. (Harry would never have been able to subject every dog in the world to his experiment.) What one tries to do, then, is come up with a collection of individuals, a part of the group, that is representative of the whole. The size of the collection would be determined by the degree of its representativeness. It has to be sufficiently large that you can be reasonably sure it contains all the variety to be found in the group as a whole.

18. Assessing Argument

By way of brief review: An argument expresses the heart of reasoning, the inferential move; in its simplest form it invites us to accept one idea as true on the basis of another. The first thing to ascertain, in assessing an argument, is whether or not there is indeed an argument to assess. In other words, are the two basic elements of argument, premises and a conclusion, present at all? Sometimes, in what superficially appears to be an argument, we have a discourse in which a point is stated vigorously, perhaps in a variety of ways, but is unaccompanied by any discernible supporting data. Only a supported statement is worthy of the term "conclusion." An unsupported statement is a mere opinion, which we are free to take or leave at face value.

Once we are confident we are dealing with a bona fide argument, we would want to look immediately to the premises that support its conclusion. First and foremost, are the premises true? This question cannot always be answered with a flat yes or no. During the normal course of events, we will come across few arguments whose premises are patently false. But often the most seductive arguments are those whose premises, while not out-and-out false, deal with the truth in such a way that it is appreciably falsified. This is when we have to be especially alert to the subtleties of language.

After we are assured we are dealing with true premises, we need to test their strength in terms of their relevancy to the conclusion they seek to support. The next thing we have to determine is whether or not the argument is structurally sound. Does it in fact make critical connections between the ideas on which the soundness of its conclusion depends? If an argument purports to be advancing a conclusion that follows necessarily, when in fact it does not, the argument fails. In arguments advancing probable conclusions, the degree of the probable truth of those conclusions depends on the degree to which the data constituting the premises of an argument lend strong and convincing support to the claims made by the conclusion.

In the final analysis, the force of an argument depends on the extent to which it reflects the objective order of things. We argue well because first we reason well, and the purpose of both arguing and reasoning is to enable us to perform more freely and purposefully in the world.

19. Constructing an Argument

In constructing an argument, the first thing to be mindful of is the two basic elements of argument: premises and a conclusion. You will not end up with an argument if you simply make statements. Your statements must be such that some of them (the premises) serve as the supporting data for another statement (the conclusion). Focus your attention on the premises. You are, presumably, clear as to the point you want to make (the conclusion). The question is: Do the premises show that it is reasonable to accept the conclusion, either as a necessary truth or a highly probable one? Your premises must measure up with respect to two counts, truth and strength.

THE TRUTH OF PREMISES

That premises must be true is obvious. Only someone who deliberately sets out to deceive would put forward a premise that is blatantly false. But it is not always a matter of either blatantly false or brilliantly true. A premise may be substantially true but not precisely true. If you have the least doubt about any of the evidence you are going to use in an argument, check it out beforehand. This is where getting the facts straight is of paramount importance. Single statements that make several claims must of course be wholly true, not just true in part. If you state in an argument on behalf of a senatorial candidate that "Stephens served in Vietnam as a Marine and earned the Purple Heart there," and an enterprising investigative reporter discovers that, though Stephens indeed served in Vietnam, he was neither a Marine nor earned a Purple Heart, your whole argument will be called into question, and justly so.

A particular statement might be perfectly true, yet be expressed in such a way that its truth is not readily evident to an audience. Hence the importance of clear, cogent language. If you are trying to communicate to a British audience that Burns is a native of the state of Ohio and you tell them "Burns is a Buckeye from birth," there is a strong likelihood that they will not get the message.

THE STRENGTH OF PREMISES

As we have seen, a premise might be true but not have an immediate bearing on the conclusion it is attempting to support. A relevant premise is one which most directly supports a conclusion. If you come up with several premises to support a certain conclusion, you will not necessarily have a more compelling argument if you choose to use all of them. They will surely not all support the conclusion with the same kind of directness. Weed out the weaker premises; otherwise they will only divert attention from the stronger ones.

Even in an instance when you have several premises, all of which, say, effectively support your conclusion because of their directness, it is best not to use all of them. Limiting the number of premises gives your argument sharper focus and therefore greater impact. Another consideration: Certain premises (reasons for accepting the conclusion) might carry more weight with a specific kind of audience. It is just those premises, then, that you should employ with that audience.

That last point calls to mind a time-honored admonition: Know your audience. In this regard, it is well to remember that, while logic is a science, it is also an art. An argument has a dual purpose: to produce true conclusions and to persuade an audience. To succeed in the latter we have to present our argument in a way that suits the audience in front of us. That's where the artistry comes in.

PART FOUR

The Sources of Illogical Thinking

M istakes in reasoning may be merely accidental, or, more seriously, the result of carelessness. More seriously yet, they may proceed from attitudes or set points of view that are themselves conducive to illogical thinking. In this part of the book I survey some of the attitudes and points of view that are consciously to be avoided because they inhibit our ability to think logically.

1. Skepticism

There is a place for skepticism in sound reasoning, but it should be selectively employed. A distinction has to be made between skepticism as a permanent attitude, which is to be avoided at all costs, and skepticism as a fitting, even necessary, response to a particular situation. In genuinely doubtful situations, we should respond with doubt. Selective skepticism is merely a matter of reserving judgment until we have sufficient information at hand to judge responsibly. For example, we should be reluctant to accept the conclusion of an argument whose premises, for one reason or another, are questionable. This kind of healthy skepticism is preserving of sound reasoning.

But skepticism as a permanent attitude, a philosophical point of view, is deadly. It subverts the reasoning process before it even gets started, transforming it into a process of mis-reasoning. There are two expressions of the skeptical attitude, one more extreme than the other, but both equally damaging. The extreme skeptic proclaims baldly that there is no truth. This is obviously a self-contradictory position, for if there is no truth there is no standard by which that very claim can be assessed, and the skeptic's statement is empty of meaning. The moderate skeptic is prepared to concede that truth may exist, but he maintains that if it does, the human mind is incapable of attaining it. At first, this position might appear less dismissive of truth than that of the extreme skeptic, but it really is not. A truth that is merely theoretical, and to which we do not have access, is, for all practical purposes, nonexistent.

Logic, as we said at the very outset, is essentially about truth. If truth is but a fleeting sprite we can only chase but never catch, logic is not worth bothering about, for in that case human reasoning would amount to little more than an exercise in futility.

2. Evasive Agnosticism

An agnostic is someone who maintains that he lacks enough knowledge regarding a particular issue to be able to make a definite judgment about it. The term is usually applied to religious belief. Whereas an atheist states categorically that there is no God, an agnostic says he does not know whether or not there is a God. But an agnostic attitude can be taken toward any subject, not just religion. There is a marked difference between the skeptic and the agnostic. The agnostic, unlike the skeptic, neither denies the existence of truth nor its attainability. He simply claims ignorance as to the truth of a certain matter. Just as there is a place for skepticism in sound reasoning, so is there also a place for an honest agnosticism. We are being honestly agnostic when we simply admit to an ignorance that is really ours, here and now. If our knowledge of a particular thing is so limited that it does not allow us to take a confident position regarding it, we should refrain from committing ourselves. To do otherwise would be intellectually irresponsible. Evasive agnosticism is the attitude that attempts to pass off vincible ignorance as if it were invincible. It is one thing to say "I don't know" after long and assiduous research into a subject. It is quite another to say "I don't know" when you haven't even bothered to look into the matter. The person who succumbs to evasive agnosticism uses ignorance as an excuse rather than a reason. Such ignorance is the result of indifference or laziness.

3. Cynicism and Naïve Optimism

A cynic is someone who makes emphatically negative estimates without sufficient evidence. A naïve optimist is someone who makes emphatically positive estimates without sufficient evidence. Both represent illogical positions. Both the cynic and the naïve optimist act out of prejudice (the word comes from the Latin *praejudicare*, "to judge beforehand"), because they make up their mind about a particular matter before it has been fully encountered and seriously engaged with, not to say intelligently assimilated. A cynic preparing for a debate will assume a) the issues to be debated are ridiculous, b) his opponent is a fool, and c) no good what-ever will come from the debate itself. The problem with cynicism, apart from its intrinsic illogicality, is that it blinds us to possibilities, and very often transforms our negative estimates and expectations into self-fulfilling prophecies.

A naïve optimist, after spending an hour with a young woman whom he has just met for the first time, is convinced that she has a) the beauty of Helen of Troy, b) the intelligence of Madame Curie, and c) the artistic prowess of Emily Dickinson. Naïve optimism, besides giving us a skewed view of the present, sets us up for future disappointment, for things are rarely as the naïve optimist supposes them to be. Neither the cynic nor the naïve optimist is paying the right kind of attention to the world around himself. Rather than seeing things as they are, he sees them as he is predisposed to see them.

4. Narrow-Mindedness

The college president's wife has lost a pearl earring of inestimable value somewhere within the confines of the football field. You are going to search for it. But you have decided beforehand, in a purely arbitrary fashion, that in conducting your search you will limit yourself to a ten-yard-wide strip in the middle of the field. By narrowing the scope of your search in that way, you will be ignoring 90 percent of the area in which the earring might be found. Your chances of ever finding it are reduced accordingly.

We say that the whole purpose of logic, of sound reasoning, is to discover the truth. Because the exact whereabouts of something is obviously not known until after it is discovered, we have to keep our minds open beforehand to a variety of possibilities. People are not to be considered narrow-minded simply because they limit the scope of their inquiry, for that is a practical necessity which avoids wasted effort. A narrow-minded person refuses to consider certain alternatives only because they do not meet his prejudiced assumptions about what is and is not worth pursuing. The limiting process lacks a rational basis, in other words. Narrow-mindedness is clearly debilitating in its effects, but there is a certain kind of open-mindedness which may be even more so. G. K. Chesterton pointedly observed that an open mind, like an open mouth, should eventually close on something. A healthy open-mindedness does not mean that one is indiscriminately open to everything. To be noncommittal in a situation that demands commitment is no virtue. To be tolerant of everything is to value nothing. And, from a purely practical point of view, the search for truth necessitates our imposing judicious limitations on the area we will investigate, so as not to expend time and energy needlessly.

5. Emotion and Argument

There is a basic truth of human psychology that one does not have to learn from a textbook: The more intense our emotional state, the more difficult it is to think clearly and behave temperately. A person in the throes of violent anger is seldom a paragon of rationality. We have to exert conscious effort to keep emotion out of argument. We will never succeed completely at this, and in fact it would not be a good thing were we to do so, but we need to be constantly aware of the fact that if emotion gains the ascendancy in any situation, clear thinking is going to suffer.

We are by nature emotional creatures, and to imagine that we could completely divest ourselves of our emotions— even temporarily, while we are engaged in argument— would be unrealistic. Though some ancient philosophers looked upon emotion and reason as inhabiting separate realms, with open belligerence between them, in fact the two inhabit the same domain and, ideally at least, should get along harmoniously. An idea, even of the most rarefied sort, is never devoid of emotion, for every idea is the brainchild of that naturally emotional creature who is man.

It is a matter of putting the emphasis on reason, then, and not of attempting to exclude emotion entirely. What should move people in a sound argument is its intellectual substance, the ideas and their interconnections—and not whatever emotional overtones the argument may carry with it. A conclusion should be accepted not because we feel good about it but because we see that it is true and therefore worthy of our acceptance. There is a simple rule of thumb to be followed here: *Never appeal directly to people's emotions.* Devote your efforts to bringing them to the point where they can see for themselves what is the case. The only thing really worth feeling good about is the truth.

6. *The Reason for Reasoning*

Reasoning can be employed for an unspecifiable number of purposes, both good and bad. Some of history's most notorious criminals have been possessed of finely tuned logical minds, logical in the sense that they reasoned consistently from the presuppositions with which they began.

The problem was that the presuppositions with which they began were false. In this little book we have been advocating a view of logic that regards it as more than mere consistent reasoning. To be consistent in one's thinking if one's thinking is askew (i.e., not consistent with the objective order of things) is not to be logical, in the right understanding of the term, for logic has essentially to do with the truth. To use reasoning for any purpose other than attaining the truth is to misuse it. The ideal implied in that assertion is a very high one, and our record for living up to it is not admirable. But ideals are about the what-should-be.

It is at times too easy to be so governed by our emotions in our reasoning that argument becomes primarily a means of venting our anger, or of vindicating ourselves, or of getting even, or of simply scoring points for the sake of self-aggrandizement. The truth is thus relegated to incidental status. In the ideal debate, the primary purpose of the debaters is not to triumph over each other, but rather by their combined efforts to ferret out the truth as it pertains to the issues being debated. As for winning at all costs? "At all costs" is a price no one can afford.

7. Argumentation Is Not Quarreling

Argument is rational discourse. It is not to be confused with quarreling. The object of argument is to get at the truth. The object of quarreling is to get at other people. There are any number of folk who, though happy to quarrel with you, are either unwilling or unable to *argue* with you. Do not waste time and energy trying to argue with people who will not or cannot argue.

8. The Limits of Sincerity

Sincerity is a necessary condition for sound reasoning but not a sufficient one. If you do not regard a position that you publicly advocate, and are willing to defend in argument, as true, you are abusing reason. Who wants to argue with someone who doesn't really believe in what he is saying? And what is more exasperating, after a long and spirited argument in defense of something you passionately believe in, than to learn that your interlocutor, defending the opposite position, was arguing just for the sake of argument? Only a sentimentalist believes that sincerity alone is enough. In fact, utter sincerity may combine perfectly with undeniable error. I can be utterly sincere and dead wrong. My sincerity cannot transform falsehood into truth. Of course, one *must* be sincere. But one must also be right.

9. Common Sense

Logic, though more than common sense, is born out of it. Success in logical thinking, then, and in the avoidance of illogical thinking, is rooted in a respect for common sense. Common sense is that homey everyday-type reasoning which is born out of an alert awareness of, and respect for, the obvious. It is characterized by the unfailing capacity consistently to distinguish between a cat and a kangaroo. Common sense looks upon language as principally a means of revealing things, not concealing them, and is suspicious of words that dazzle more than denote. Common sense sticks close to the basics and renders to the first principles of reason the reverence they deserve. It is "common" sense in that it is shared by all those animals whom Aristotle defined as rational.

PART FIVE

The Principal Forms of Illogical Thinking

Theoretically, the number of ways reasoning can go awry is beyond reckoning, but specific mistakes in reasoning tend to group themselves into a limited number of typical patterns. The various typical patterns of mis-reasoning are called "fallacies." There are two basic types of fallacies, the formal and the informal. "Formal fallacies" deal with the form, or the structure, of argument. "Informal fallacies" deal with every kind of logical mistake other than formal ones. In what follows we will deal with the most important types of both types of fallacies, beginning with the formal.

One who is attempting to master logical thinking might suppose that becoming familiar with the ways in which reasoning can go wrong is not of much benefit, or, worse, that it may actually be counterproductive. Neither supposition is correct. Primary emphasis must be given to the positive principles, of course, but knowledge of the pitfalls of reasoning has a twofold benefit: 1) it brings into greater relief the correct ways of reasoning, sharpening our sense of them, and thus enables us to be more surely guided by them; 2) it protects us against being victimized by bad reasoning whenever we find ourselves on the receiving end of it.

It is particularly important to note that fallacious reasoning can often be very persuasive, sometimes more so than sound reasoning. Therein lies its great danger. The principal explanation for this is that a favorite tactic of fallacious reasoning is to circumvent sound reasoning by appealing directly to the emotions.

1. Denying the Antecedent

In discussing conditional argument (of the form $A \rightarrow B$), we saw that there were two valid modes, affirming the antecedent and denying the consequent. Matching those valid modes are two invalid ones, the first of which is "denying the antecedent." Here is the pattern of the argument:

$A \rightarrow B$
-A
Therefore, -B

And here is the argument in English:

If Louise is running, then she is moving.
Louise is not running.
Therefore, she is not moving.

COMMENT: We can see clearly that the fact that Louise is not running does not necessarily mean that she is not moving. What the major premise tells us is that if A comes about, B will necessarily come about (Louise can't be running while not moving), but it does not say that A is the only condition that can be met in order to produce B. (Louise can be moving because she is walking, or rolling over in her sleep, or rocking in a rocking chair.) This being the case, the mere absence of A does not allow us to conclude that B will also be absent. Remember, this is an *invalid* argument because the conclusion does not follow *necessarily*. Could the conclusion possibly be true? It could be, but we don't know for certain.

2. Affirming the Consequent

The second invalid mode of conditional argument is called "affirming the consequent," and here it is expressed symbolically:

> A → B
> B
> Therefore, A

And in English:

> If Louise is running, then she is moving.
> Louise is moving.
> Therefore, she is running.

COMMENT: Immediately we can see that the conclusion does not follow. Why not? Let's go back to the major premise. It tells us that a specific condition must be met (Louise's running) in order for a specific consequent to follow (her moving). As noted with regard to the previous argument, the statement does not say that this is the *only* condition which, being met, will necessitate the consequent. Thus, if the consequent is in place (Louise's moving), we cannot conclude that the only possible explanation for its being so is this specific condition (Louise's running).

There are any number of other ways that Louise could be moving besides running. Again, the conclusion might be true, but it is not necessarily so.

3. The Undistributed Middle Term

In our discussion of syllogistic argument, we saw that the middle term (the term appearing in the premises but not in the conclusion) must be a universal term (distributed) at least once in order for it to have the proper scope to make the connection between the major term and the minor term. If this fails to happen, we have the formal fallacy called the "undistributed middle term." A less technical name given to this fallacy is "guilt by association." We can see the pertinence of the latter name in this example:

> Several Nazis were members of the Kaiser Club.
> Hans was a member of the Kaiser Club.
> Therefore, Hans was a Nazi.

COMMENT: This is fallacious reasoning because, contrary to what the conclusion asserts, it does not follow that just because Hans belonged to a club that had Nazi members he was himself a Nazi. This circumstance might raise certain suspicions about Hans, but it does not allow us to proclaim as a fact what can be at best only conjecture.

4. Equivocation

An equivocal term or word has more than a single meaning. The potential problem that can be caused by equivocal terms is ambiguity. If we unintentionally create ambiguity by the way we use language, there is no question of our committing a fallacy. The fallacy occurs when we deliberately employ words with multiple meanings for the purpose of deception.

In our discussion of syllogistic argument, we saw that one of the requirements for the validity of the argument is that it have three terms and three terms only. It would seem that avoiding the error of having a syllogism with four terms would be quite easy, since all one would have to do is count up one's terms. But the error becomes less readily detectable if one of the terms in the syllogism is being used equivocally. On the surface, the argument (expressed symbolically) would look like this:

$$M—P$$
$$\frac{S—M}{S—P}$$

But because one of the terms, M, is being used in two quite different ways, the argument in effect contains four terms and is therefore invalid. When the symbolically expressed argument reflects the equivocation, the error becomes obvious:

$$M—P$$
$$\frac{S—Q}{S—P}$$

Consider the following argument:

Fans make a lot of noise.
Madame Butterfly was using her fan.
Therefore, she was making a lot of noise.

COMMENT: "Fan" here is being used, rather heavy-handedly, in two ways. In the major premise it refers to sports fans of some kind or another. In the minor premise it refers to the instrument with which, by waving it back and forth, we create a breeze and cool ourselves. The conscious use of equivocation need not always be malicious. It is commonly used to bring about an intentionally humorous effect.

Consider the following argument. Here the equivocation is a bit more subtle.

> Loving one's neighbor is a mark of altruism.
> Don Juan was a great lover.
> It follows that he was an altruist.

COMMENT: The problem here is "love," potentially a very ambiguous word, given the many meanings that can be assigned to it. The major premise gives us a reasonable and readily acceptable understanding of love. It reflects the classic definition of love as willing the good for the other. The minor premise, on the other hand, gives us a more popular, even vulgar understanding of love. When we say that Don Juan was a great lover, what we mean, in effect, is that he was a philanderer, which is not quite the same thing as an altruist.

The conclusion does not follow, because the love at which Don Juan was so adept was not the same kind of love we equate with altruism. Don Juan and altruism cannot be connected, because there is not a single middle term to make that connection. If the premises are stated in terms of what they actually mean, a meaning that is disguised by the equivocation, we can see that no conclusion is possible.

> Love of neighbor is a mark of altruism.
> Don Juan was a philanderer.

Clearly, there's nowhere to go from here. The words that lend themselves to equivocation, intentional or not, are those to which many meanings can, and regularly are, attached. If you plan to argue a point about justice, say, make sure you begin by giving a precise definition of the term, and then consistently stick with that definition throughout the argument.

5. Begging the Question

The rationale behind an argument, as we know, is to prove a point. The burden placed upon the one making the argument, then, is to provide concrete evidence on the basis of which the conclusion can be seen to be true. The fallacy we call "begging the question" is therefore a very basic kind of mistake, for it attempts to get around the whole argumentative process. A discourse that commits this fallacy might superficially appear to be an argument but in fact it is not.

The reason is that it lacks real premises—information that offers genuine support for the conclusion. The specific mark of the fallacy is this: The very point that has to be proved to be true is simply assumed to be true. Consider the following argument:

> Because Shirley is given to prevarication,
> Shirley is a liar.

We might too quickly suppose we have a genuine argument here with a real conclusion, because the first statement seems to serve as a premise for the second. But if we reflect on what that first statement says, we see that it is simply repeating, using different words, what the conclusion says. The two statements differ only verbally, not in terms of their content. So, the very point that needs to be proved is assumed to be true, without there being offered any substantiation for it. Let's consider a more complicated form of the fallacy:

> All the people at the table had their heads shaved.
> Jim was at the table.
> Therefore, Jim had his head shaved.

Again, superficially considered, the conclusion of this discourse might appear to be *demonstrating* something to be true, but that is not the case. If we reflect on the first statement, which has all the marks of a bona fide major premise, we see that the only way it could be made would be on the basis of a prior knowledge of the conclusion. I could not know that "all" the people at the table had their heads shaved if I didn't already know that Jim had his head shaved. So the conclusion merely repeats information that we already know. No real inference is being made here.

A variation of the begging-the-question fallacy is "arguing in a circle," sometimes called the "vicious circle." The gist of the fallacy is this: First, one statement A is used as the supporting premise for another statement B; then, later, the process is reversed, and what was initially the premise A now becomes the conclusion, and the original conclusion B serves as the premise. Consider the following argument (I will label the statements so the reversal will stand out):

A) Because human beings are entirely determined

B) They lack free will.

Then, a few pages later, we read:

B) Given the fact that human beings lack free will

A) It follows that they are entirely determined in their actions.

If the two arguments were put right next to each other their circularity would be readily apparent. They are therefore separated by enough intervening prose that readers can be expected to have forgotten the first argument by the time they get to the second.

6. False Assumptions

To assume something is true is to take it to be true without being positively certain it is. There is nothing intrinsically invidious in this. Sometimes we need to assume that certain things are true in order to get the reasoning process off the ground. If the process is successful it often allows us to confirm as actually being true what we had initially *assumed* to be true. A test of a reputable assumption is that its statement does not violate the principle of contradiction. It is not patently absurd, in other words.

But assumptions must be made with great caution. A false assumption is such because it can be independently demonstrated to be false. The facts are clearly stacked against it. If one begins an argument with a false assumption, one's conclusion can only be false.

There is another kind of false assumption that can adversely affect an argument, but in a less direct way. If, in making an argument, you assume that your audience has a knowledge of a certain kind when in fact it doesn't, then its ability to follow your argument will obviously be hampered. Rule of thumb: Make as few assumptions as possible.

7. *The Straw-Man Fallacy*

In argumentation one addresses the argument, not the person behind the argument. But one must address the argument as given. If, in responding to an argument, I deliberately distort it so as to weaken it, then I commit the "straw-man fallacy." The image tells the story: A straw man is easy to deal with, a pushover. We do not commit this fallacy every time we get someone's argument wrong. Some arguments are complicated, and we can make honest mistakes in interpretation. The commission of the fallacy is a *dishonest* mistake because it is the deliberate distortion of another's argument.

8. *Using and Abusing Tradition*

Traditional practices are established ways of doing things. Established ways of doing things are commendable and worth continuing if they can stand on their own merits. Tradition, taken as a whole, might be regarded as an elaborate set of precedents. The mere fact that "things have always been done that way" is not in and of itself a compelling reason for keeping on doing them that way. It all depends on what is actually being done. Habit is a powerful influence in our lives, and we can become habituated to ways of doing things that are not intrinsically worthwhile. In evaluating a given practice, we have to keep our attention focused on the practice, not on its history.

But there is an opposite kind of mistake we can make with respect to tradition. If it is illogical to single out the longevity of a practice as the sole reason for continuing it, it is just as illogical to cite the practice's longevity as the sole reason for abandoning it. The attitude behind this mistake is a certain type of modernist thinking which assumes that only the new is worthwhile and that the only permanency we should commit ourselves to is the permanency of change. A practice is not necessarily a bad practice because it has a history behind it. Indeed, it is conceivable that the best explanation for its endurance is its intrinsic worth.

9. *Two Wrongs Don't Make a Right*

We intuitively see the illogic of the statement that two wrongs make a right. What two wrongs make, in fact, is two wrongs. The fallacy in question, put in the simplest terms, could be expressed as follows: "It is all right to do _____ because _____ has already been done." The blanks can be, and have been, filled in with selections from a full panoply of human behavior, from the innocuous to the grossly criminal.

The reasoning behind the argument rests on the assumption that precedent alone justifies future action. But precedent in and of itself provides emphatically insufficient justification for action. The fact that an act has been performed by others is of historical interest only. In deciding upon its appropriateness, we must concentrate our attention on the nature of the act itself.

All quite obvious. However, when it comes to fallacies, the obviousness of the mis-reasoning they embody has shown itself to be no sure defense against succumbing to that mis-reasoning. The pages of history are replete with examples of this fallacy, often committed on the grandest scale. "They did it first, therefore it's all right for us to pay them back in kind." But if "it" was wrong for them, it does not suddenly become right when we become the perpetrators.

10. The Democratic Fallacy

That a majority of the population in a given society holds a particular opinion on a given matter is interesting sociological information, but it has no necessary bearing on the truth or falsity of the matter in question. Majorities can be wrong. They can also be right. The "democratic fallacy" is the assumption that the mere fact that most people *believe* proposition X to be true is sufficient evidence to allow us to conclude that proposition X *is* true.

If most people in a society are of the opinion that black is white and white is black, alas for the opinion of most people in that society. Whether something is black or white is not a matter of subjective opinion but of objective fact. That much being said, it has to be acknowledged that on an emotional level, the democratic fallacy can be very persuasive. As many great figures in history have found out, it is not easy to stand up against the crowd when the crowd holds black to be white and white to be black.

11. The Ad Hominem Fallacy

To repeat an important rule: In argumentation we respond to the argument, not to the person behind the argument. That rule is broken when the argument is ignored and the person responsible for the argument is deliberately attacked. When that happens the "ad hominem fallacy" is being committed. (*Ad hominem*, in Latin, means "against the person.") The thrust of this illogical ploy is the making public of certain negative information about the personal life of one's opponent that, though irrelevant to the issues being argued, is emotionally volatile. The intention of the perpetrator of this fallacy is to divert an audience's attention from the argument, usually because the perpetrator is getting the worst of it.

If my only purpose is to win an argument, the ad hominem fallacy can effectively advance that cause. It can turn an audience against my opponent, but for reasons irrelevant to the argument; through it I can find favor with the audience, for reasons similarly irrelevant. In the aftermath I might congratulate myself that I won the argument, but that is precisely what I did not do—not in any logical sense, at any rate. My dubious victory was not based on the merits of my ideas, but on my ability to prevent the argument of my opponent from getting a fair hearing.

12. Substituting for the Force of Reason

The ideal argument allows people to see that something is true on the basis of evidence. The only force that an honest arguer wants to use is the force of reason.

The alternative to moving people by force of reason is doing so by raw power. People can be forced to do what they do not want to do, but they cannot be forced to think what they do not want to think. They cannot be coerced into accepting what is true. In argument, coercion invariably backfires. People will accept the truth only when they can do so freely, having seen for themselves that what is presented as true is in fact true.

13. The Uses and Abuses of Expertise

An expert is an authority in a specific field. It is perfectly legitimate, in argument, to appeal to the views of experts if they are relevant to the point one is attempting to establish. But certain precautions must be taken in following this practice. Consider this argument:

> Professor Smith says the Acme Program is good.
> Professor Jones says the Acme Program is good.
> Professor Doe says the Acme Program is good.
> Therefore, we should adopt the Acme Program.

Let us say that the three professors cited here are all genuine experts in the field to which the Acme Program relates. That is, their testimony qualifies as relevant. But let us say further that none of the professors offers us any reasons why he believes the program is good. The professors make no argument. The program is to be adopted merely on their say-so.

But it is argument, not just the word of the experts, which should be carrying the authoritative weight, and the argument we are presented with here is far from convincing, because it offers us nothing beyond the mere word of the experts. If we are satisfied with only the word of the experts, we are essentially being told: "Don't ask any questions, just do as we say."

The strongest kind of expert evidence incorporates the reasons the experts advance for holding a certain position. In such a case, we have more than mere opinion to deal with.

Just as we have to examine our own assertions to make sure they square with the facts, so too we have to make sure the expert evidence we use in an argument is truly that. There are many people who pass themselves off as experts but who don't qualify as such. The test here is not what people say about what they know, but how they show what they know through argument.

Needless to say, the pronouncements of a bona fide expert are worth paying attention to only insofar as they pertain to areas in which that expertise has been established. This fairly obvious point bears mentioning only because it is frequently overlooked. The views of a world-famous musician on subjects such as the economy or global warming carry no special weight if the only authority behind them is the musician's musical accomplishments.

14. *The Quantifying of Quality*

We regularly express quality in quantitative terms, a practice that can bring with it considerable practical benefits, but we should be aware of its limitations. Heat is a quality.

We quantify it. Yesterday's high temperature was reported to be ninety-three degrees Fahrenheit, and other numbers pertaining to the humidity index and wind velocity were thrown into the mix. Let us say that the numbers for temperature and humidity are higher today than they were yesterday, and there is no wind. But for some reason it doesn't feel as hot today as it did yesterday. One might suppose that one should feel hotter today because the numbers representing the heat read higher today than they did yesterday, but that would be true only if quality could be perfectly translated into quantity. That such is not the case is shown by the fact that my experiences are at odds with the reading on the thermometer.

In the strictest sense, no quality can be quantified, since if quality could be perfectly translated into quantity there would be no basis for the distinction between the two in the first place. We speak of the color blue in terms of certain frequencies of light waves, but when we have the experience of seeing blue it is not light waves we are seeing, but blue. The experience of numbers is not the same kind of experience as that of the qualities to which numbers can be attached. We indulge in a false sense of precision if we suppose we know a quality better, as a quality, because it has been quantified.

Many important things do not submit themselves to quantitative assessment; perhaps we would want to say the most important things do not. Consider love, beauty, kindness, justice, freedom, and peace. How does one measure them? What is their mass and velocity? How much do they cost in dollars and cents? To attempt to quantify something that doesn't lend itself to quantification is to distort it.

15. *Consider More Than the Source*

Let us say that you are the personnel officer for a prestigious firm. As part of your job, you have developed a pretty good working knowledge of the prominent colleges and universities around the country and the kinds of graduates they typically turn out. In particular, you know that Vacuous U is a very sorry excuse for an academic institution. You are seeking to fill an important position in your firm and are taking applications. Having just glanced at the application submitted by a graduate of Vacuous U, one Peter Petri, you promptly decide, simply on the basis of the candidate's being a graduate of that institution, to reject the application. You have just committed a fallacy.

It is not that your decision was completely unreasonable. After all, given what you know about Vacuous U, it is probable that Mr. Petri is not an especially strong candidate. But there is no necessity there. It is possible that a genuinely sparkling individual could emerge even from an unillustrious academic institution such as Vacuous U. The essence of the fallacy you committed is this: Knowing a source to be generally bad, you assume that everything coming from that source must necessarily be bad. This doesn't follow.

Certainly it is relevant to consider the source of something or someone whose qualities we are assessing. But we must go beyond that. First question: Where does Mr. Petri come from? Next and much more germane question: Taken in himself, what are Mr. Petri's qualities?

16. Stopping Short at Analysis

Because we are by nature analytic creatures, we have to take things apart, mentally if not physically, in order fully to understand them. But analysis is only productive if it is complemented by synthesis. It is not enough to take things apart; we have to put them back together again.

Ed likes to dismantle cars. He has succeeded in taking any number of them apart, but to date he has not managed to put one back together again and get it running. From this we can confidently conclude that Ed doesn't really know all that much about cars. He can analyze them, but he can't synthesize them.

The purpose of analysis is not simply to know the individual parts that make up a thing but to know how they relate to one another—to know how, taken together, they constitute a whole. Regarded in purely quantitative terms, a whole is no more than the sum of its parts. But if that view were adequate to understanding the nature of a thing, then the dismantled parts of a clock, gathered together in one place, would be a clock and would behave accordingly.

17. Reductionism

A composed thing, as just noted, is always more than the parts of which it is composed. For instance, the human body can be analyzed in terms of the chemical elements that make it up, but to argue that the human body is no more than a collection of chemicals is to succumb to crudely simplistic reasoning, and to commit the fallacy of "reductionism."

This fallacy is committed when we selectively focus on only some of the parts of a composed whole. This is what we do when we call attention exclusively to negative traits of a person and then pretend that in doing so we have revealed what the person, as a person, is really all about.

18. Misclassification

If we are naturally analytic creatures, we are naturally classifying creatures as well. We come to know things more fully by associating them with other things, specifically by grouping them together with other things they are similar to. (You will recall that this is the first step in the process of logical definition.) The misclassification of things—taking an apple for an orange—can have serious consequences. A book incorrectly cataloged in a large library may be effectively lost for years. We misclassify things because we fail to properly identify them in the first place, and we do that because we are not paying attention.

19. The Red Herring

There are several fallacies whose effective purpose is to make us miss the point, and they do this by diverting our attention from the issues at hand. We have already seen this in the ad hominem fallacy, which occurs when we introduce emotionally volatile information having to do with the person of our opponent that is completely irrelevant to the argument. The "red-herring fallacy" provides us with another example of this tactic. It introduces emotionally volatile information which is deliberately calculated to agitate a specific audience. Two things make this tactic fallacious: First, it is a direct appeal to emotion, not reason; second, the information introduced has nothing at all to do with the issues being dealt with in the argument.

Louis and Lawrence are chemists who are debating whether their company should introduce a new line of fertilizer. They are debating before one of the departments in the company whose members were recently denied a requested pay raise. Louis, who developed the new fertilizer, is ardently committed to its being put on the market. But he senses he is not doing well in the debate, and in fact it looks as if Lawrence's opposing arguments will prevail. Desperate, he introduces the subject of the recently denied pay raise. As a result, near pandemonium breaks out. The debate abruptly comes to an end. The subject of the pay raise was unmistakably a red herring.

20. Laughter as Diversionary Tactic

We fall into this fallacy when, unable to come up with a reasoned response to an argument, we try to dodge it by pretending that it is not worth taking seriously. We might go so far as to contend that it is no more than a laughing matter. Getting people to laugh at an argument can serve as a powerful way of dismissing it, but this may have nothing to do with the intrinsic worth of the argument. If a devious debator cannot get an audience to laugh at an argument, he might try to turn his opponent into a laughingstock, say by calling attention to some irrelevancy like a speech impediment, and thereby divert attention away from an argument he cannot handle.

To be sure, there are arguments that are comically inept and therefore deserving of laughter. But even in those cases it is better, rather than dismissing an argument with easy ridicule, to take the time to show how and why it fails as an argument.

21. Tears as Diversionary Tactic

Besides using laughter to get an argument off track, we can also do so by playing on the sympathies of an audience. The fallacy here involves deliberately obscuring issues through the cynical manipulation of emotion.

Arguments frequently deal with emotionally charged issues. It is especially important, when such is the case, to exert more than ordinary efforts to keep emotion under control. Given the inverse relation between the presence of intense emotions and the ability to think clearly, if emotion is allowed to take over, the chances of conducting a persuasive argument are next to nil.

We succumb to this fallacy when we intentionally ignore or downplay the pertinent issues at hand, focusing on matters either peripheral or irrelevant to the argument and appealing directly to the emotions of the audience in an attempt to gain its sympathy. Let us say that I have been invited to address a town-hall meeting to express my views on a proposed tax hike for education. I am very much against the tax hike. Once I am at the podium, instead of giving my attention to the principal purpose of the meeting, I spend all my time theatrically lamenting the woes I had to suffer during my student days in the local school system. By that diversionary tactic I manage to win the emotional support of my audience, and gain many "no" votes against the tax hike.

22. *An Inability to Disprove Does Not Prove*

The fact that there is no concrete proof against a position does not constitute an argument in favor of the position. I cannot claim to be right simply because you can't prove me to be wrong. Consider the following exchange:

> Dr. Willing: We are not alone in the universe. I maintain
> that there is intelligent life out there in the vast
> reaches of space.
> Dr. Able: Do you have proof of this?
> Dr. Willing: I don't. But can you prove there is *not* life in
> outer space?
> Dr. Able: No, I cannot.
> Dr. Willing: Aha! That proves I am right.

COMMENT: Dr. Willing is attempting to close prematurely a question that remains open. Because there is no proof for or against the question of whether there is life in outer space, proponents of either side cannot claim that lack of proof for the position they oppose stands as proof of the position they favor.

23. *The False Dilemma*

Our English word "dilemma" comes from two Greek words, which can be roughly translated as "two possibilities." There are genuine either/or situations in life—situations, that is, in which there are two possibilities and only two possibilities open to us. And there are also situations in which there are several possibilities open to us.

I commit the fallacy of the false dilemma when, in a situation entailing several possibilities, I attempt to persuade you that there are only two. The dilemma is false because it represents a distortion of the actual state of affairs.

The fallacy seeks to create a false sense of urgency in an audience, to force them to choose between the alternatives carefully selected by the perpetrator of the fallacy. This sense of urgency is especially important to achieve if neither of the alternatives being offered is particularly attractive. Let us say I present you with the alternatives of A or B. I want you to choose A. Here is how I would argue: "A, admittedly, is not all that pleasant a choice, but the only alternative you have is B, and that is awful. Certainly you would not want *that*!"

24. Post Hoc Ergo Propter Hoc

The Latin name for the fallacy we will now discuss, *post hoc ergo propter hoc*, translates very straightforwardly as "after that, therefore on account of that." (The phrase itself represents a mini-argument, you will notice.) The fallacy has to do with causality. In a cause-and-effect relationship the cause is always prior to the effect, in the sense that the cause has to be present before the effect can take place. But often there is a detectable temporal priority with respect to the cause. First I light the fuse of the stick of dynamite (cause); the fuse burns down and then, after a lapse of time, there is a tremendous explosion (effect). The fallacy of *post hoc ergo propter hoc* is committed when, in response to a situation where a certain event A happens, followed by another event B, we decide, *solely on the basis of A having come before B*, that A caused B.

A caveman inclined to philosophical speculation suddenly took note of the fact that every morning as far back as he could remember, the singing of the birds invariably preceded the rising of the sun. On the basis of this evidence he happily concluded that it was the singing of the birds that caused the daily sunrise. He thus committed the *post hoc ergo propter hoc* fallacy.

The temporal precedence of one event over another is not irrelevant in considering whether there might be a causal relationship between the two, but the information is not conclusive. We need to know more. The best we can conclude, if that is all the information we have at hand, is that the first event *may* have caused the second. If our caveman had pursued his philosophical speculations further—as his progeny did—he would have discovered that the mere fact that the birds sang, then the sun rose, was not sufficient to support the conclusion that the singing caused the rising.

25. *Special Pleading*

The "fallacy of special pleading" is committed when we selectively omit significant information because it would weigh against a position we are promoting. The result of those omissions is a serious distortion of the subject under discussion.

Let us say that I am writing a history of my alma mater, Carefree College. I am genuinely devoted to Carefree, and consider the years I spent there as the best in my life. I want my history to show the world that Carefree is one of the premier academic institutions in the country. The deeper I get into my research, however, the more I discover that Carefree's past has not been particularly edifying. But that does not deter me from my original purpose, and in writing my book I decide to ignore all the negative aspects of my college's history and to focus on the positive. In taking this approach, I commit the fallacy of special pleading, and the picture of Carefree College I present to the world is a decidedly distorted one.

26. *The Fallacy of Expediency*

Efficiency alone is not enough to determine the worth of an action. The "fallacy of expediency" is committed when we ignore every aspect of a means other than its capacity to achieve a desired end. It is not enough to point to the bottom line, as if that were all that mattered. The question is: How did we get to the bottom line?

We commit this fallacy when we show ourselves willing

to adopt any tactic, however irrational, for the sole purpose of bringing about our desired ends. The governing attitude is: It doesn't matter how we get there, just so long as we get there.

27. *Avoiding Conclusions*

Human reasoning is purposeful. We think about problems to resolve them. We make arguments so that through them we can arrive at conclusions. The premises of an argument are the means by which we get to the conclusion. As we have seen, they must be adequate to the job. If we jump to a conclusion when we possess insufficient evidence (weak premises), our argument will not be compelling.

Conclusions are meant to be arrived at. Argument, as the linguistic expression of human reasoning, is goal-oriented. To suppose that we engage in argument simply to hear ourselves talk is to trivialize it. It is one thing to acknowledge there are certain problems that may be insoluble, that certain conclusions are beyond our reach. But it is quite another thing to adopt the principle that problems as such are insoluble and conclusions as such unreachable. That is to use reason to undermine the very nature of reason.

28. *Simplistic Reasoning*

If we are tempted to call black white, or white black, it is because the complexities of life sometimes overwhelm us. But it is not a rational response to a complex reality to simplify it in such a way that grossly distorts it. The result of simplistic reasoning is always distortion.

Some audiences have a refined capacity for accepting only what they want to hear. Others have a need for easy answers. It is cynical to exploit these weaknesses. Don't tell an audience what they want to hear; tell them what is true. Don't tell them something is certain if it is not. If the reality is black, say black. If the reality is white, say white. If the reality is gray, say gray. The audience may not immediately appreciate your candor, but the hope is that in the long run it will come to see that the truth is the only thing that really matters.

Afterword

Important though it is to avoid the pitfalls of poor reasoning, it is more important to concentrate our energies on mastering those positive principles that make for its happy opposite—sound reasoning. And this is where practice comes in. Logic can be perfected as an art only by our putting it to work, by regularly applying it to real-life situations. We could never complain of a lack of opportunities for doing this; all our waking hours are chock-full of situations that demand logical responses from us.

The art of logic is like no other, for it goes to the very core of what we are. The poet Pindar offers us some radical advice when he tells us to "become what you are"—by which he means "become human." If "being logical" is not exactly the sum total of "being human," it is, I like to think, a very important part of it.

Index

ABOUT THE AUTHOR

D. Q. MCINERNY, a native of Minnesota, is a professor of philosophy and logic at Our Lady of Guadalupe Seminary. The author of a book on Thomas Merton and three textbooks on philosophy, Professor McInerny lives in Lincoln, Nebraska.